I0528357

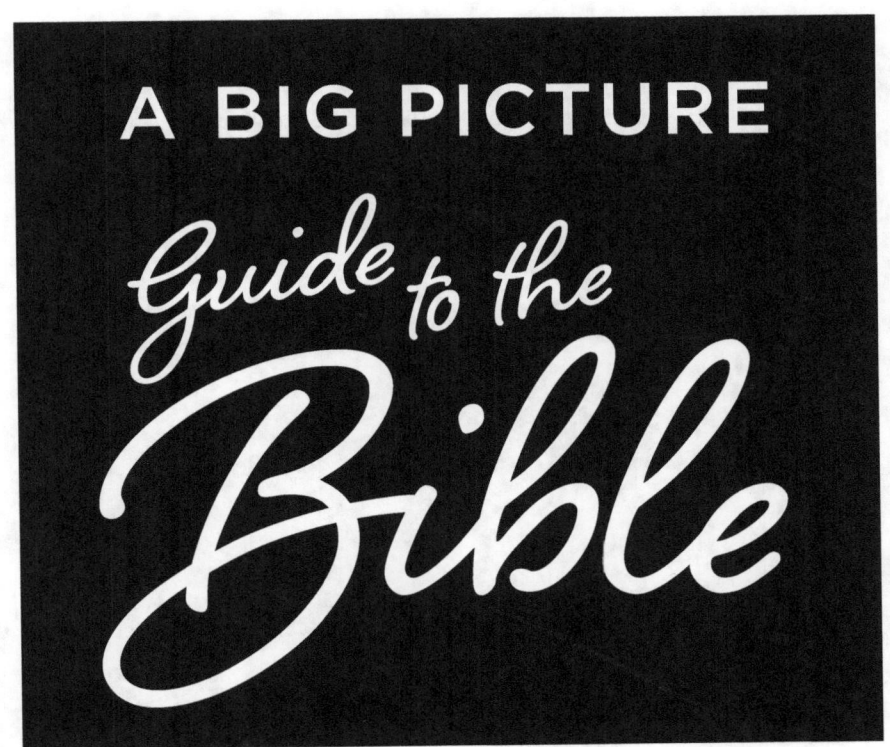

# A BIG PICTURE

## Guide to the Bible

### A FLEXIBLE INDUCTIVE STUDY OF
# HEBREWS 11

by
## PAM GILLASPIE

## Dedicated with all my love to . . .

Brad and Katie. Don't settle for the summary!

Scripture taken from the NEW
AMERICAN STANDARD BIBLE®,
© Copyright 1960, 1962, 1963, 1968,
1971, 1972, 1973, 1975, 1977, 1995 by
The Lockman Foundation.
Used by permission. (www.Lockman.org)

**A Big-Picture Guide to the Bible:
Hebrews 11**

Copyright © 2025 by Pam Gillaspie
Published by IGNITE Bible Ministries
www.pamgillaspie.com

978-1-960938-03-9

2nd edition

All rights reserved. No part of this book
may be reproduced or transmitted in
any form or by any means, electronic
or mechanical, including photocopying,
recording, or by any information storage
and retrieval system, without permission in
writing from the publisher.

Printed in the United States of America

2025

A FLEXIBLE INDUCTIVE STUDY OF

# HEBREWS 11

## Contents

In my estimation, Bible study should bring joy and life change! It should *fit* your life while simultaneously *changing* your life.

This Bible study is designed to flex with your life and give you the option to go as deep as you desire each week. If you're just starting out and feeling a little overwhelmed, stick with the main text and don't think twice about the sidebar assignments. But if you're looking for a challenge, take the sidebar prompts, roll up your sleeves, and dig to your heart's content! As you move along through the study, think of the sidebars and *Digging Deeper* boxes as the elastic that will help this study fit you perfectly.

Did you know that a little flexibility can bring a lot of joy? When a study has the ability to flex to meet you, an amazing thing happens. Guilt starts to melt away and pursuing God through His Word takes on a new sense of joy. What was once a hard obligation becomes a sweet opportunity to commune with God.

So whether you're new to the Book or have been studying it for years, this joy-based study will flex to meet you where you are and push you as far as you care to go . . . and maybe even one step further!

Life has a way of ebbing and flowing and this study is designed to ebb and flow right along with it!

***Enjoy!***

# How to use this study

This flexible inductive study will meet you where you are and take you as far as you want to go.

**1. WEEKLY STUDY:** The main text guides you through the complete topic of study for the week.

**2. FYI boxes:** For Your Information boxes provide bite-sized material to shed additional light on the topic.

> **FYI:**
>
> **Reading Tip: Begin with Prayer**
> You may have heard this a million times over and if this is a million and one, so be it. Whenever you read or study God's Word, first pray and ask His Spirit to be your Guide.

**3. ONE STEP FURTHER and other sidebar boxes:** Sidebar boxes give you the option to push yourself a little further. If you have extra time or are looking for an extra challenge, you can try one, all, or any number in between! These boxes give you the ultimate in flexibility.

> **ONE STEP FURTHER:**
>
> **Word Study: _torah_ / law**
> The first of eight Hebrew key words we encounter for God's Word is _torah_ translated "law." If you're up for a challenge this week, do a word study to learn what you can about _torah_. Run a concordance search and examine where the word _torah_ appears in the Old Testament and see what you can learn about from the contexts.
>
> If you decide to look for the word for "law" in the New Testament, you'll find that the primary Greek word is _nomos_.
>
> Be sure to see what Paul says about the law in Galatians 3 and what Jesus says in Matthew 5.

**4. DIGGING DEEPER boxes:** If you're looking to go further, Digging Deeper sections will help you sharpen your skills as you continue to mine the truths of Scripture for yourself.

> ## DIGGING DEEPER
>
> **What else does God's Word say about counselors?**
>
> If you can, spend some time this week digging around for what God's Word says about counselors.
>
> Start by considering what you already know about counsel from the Word of God and see if you can show where these truths are in the Bible. Make sure that the Word actually says what you think it says.

# The Secret to Pleasing God

*"Now faith is the assurance of things hoped for,
the conviction of things not seen."*
—Hebrews 11:1

There is nothing quite like the sinking feeling of being lost. Think for a moment how GPS has changed the way people drive. Sure we love them because they make our lives easier than maps, but they also give us that insurance against getting lost. Lost wears many faces—a toddler in a grocery store, a person behind the wheel of a small car in a big city, a teenager facing final exams only two weeks along in his reading for a 16-week class.

Lost is also the condition of many people who sit in pews around the world on any given Sunday. We're not talking theologically lost here, although some are that too; we're talking lost in regard to understanding the entire Bible. Many endure this lostness in silence not knowing quite how to correct the situation. After all, how do you "catch up" on one Book that contains 66 smaller books? A book that very few of even the most committed read through in a year. The question can be overwhelming, especially when you find yourself surrounded by others who seem to have a grip on everything you don't!

And let's be candid here: if you don't have a working knowledge of the whole Scripture, studying the parts becomes tougher—a lot tougher! But how do you acquire that working knowledge of the whole when the Bible is such a *big* book? It can be like trying to jump into the middle of *LOST* four years in. Have you ever wished God would publish a set of *Cliff's Notes* or *Spark Notes* for His Word? Something to get us up to speed on the overall message?

Well, Hebrews 11 is it! It's not the only summary God gives us in the Bible, but it is the most comprehensive and it can bring us into the flow of the story of the Bible and up to speed quickly. Does it replace reading the whole story? Of course not! But it sure will help you feel more comfortable as you gain your bearings in this epic revelation of the love of God!

FYI:

**If You're in a Class**

Complete (or at least get started on) **Lesson One** together on your first day of class. This will be a great way to start getting to know one another and will help those who are newer to Bible study get their bearings.

## CONSIDER the WAY you THINK

How well do you know the overall story of the Bible? What successes or failures have you had in Bible reading?

How have you gone about reading and/or studying?

Have you ever gotten confused by an epic or involved story anywhere else? (Think *Lord of the Rings, LOST,* etc.) If so, how did you clear things up?

How much affect does context have on understanding a story?

## OBSERVE the TEXT of SCRIPTURE

**READ** Hebrews 11 in your Bible mentally noting key words, which we'll mark later.

## DISCUSS with your GROUP or PONDER on your own . . .

What characters and events are clearly recorded in Hebrews 11?

FYI:

### The Lord of the Rings . . .

A few years back a dear missionary family lived with us for several months. We were one big happy family of four adults, six kids, three dogs, and two and a half bathrooms. The Myers love Jesus, they love people, and they love *The Lord of the Rings* books, movies, and everything else. One weekend they decided it was time to introduce our family to this epic series. I'll never forget how lost I felt for the first hour of the movie, especially as the Myers kids kept trying to bring me up to speed on who everyone was and how they were all interrelated. I thought my brain was going to explode. The only thing I even mildly connected with in the early going was the opening setting in the Shire which struck me as bearing a curious resemblance to TeleTubby land. By the end of the first movie I had enough context to enjoy the second one, but it was a hard go.

This is very similar to what happens with many of us when we try to study the Bible. We jump in with little or no context and try to figure out how everything fits into the story. More often than not, we feel like we're coming up short, and without all of the special effects wizardry we often give up quicker than we do with a movie or a television show.

Hebrews 11 is a quickstart summary, if you will, to at least bring you up to speed on many of the major players in the Bible and it is so much more worthy of your time investment than *The Lord of the Rings* (as good as it is) or perhaps the hard-to-follow mystery television shows that are coming into your mind right about now!

What other characters and events does the author allude to?

What key words did you note?

**FYI:**

**Key Words**

A key word unlocks the meaning of a text. Key words are sometimes repeated and are critical to the message of the passage. While several important words are repeated in Hebrews 11, the main key word will become obvious as you read.

## HEBREWS 11 as a SUMMARY of GOD's STORY

While there is no way to glean the overall message of the Bible without reading the whole Bible, the book of Hebrews is about as close as it gets. We've already talked about Hebrews 11 as a chapter that gives us a quick overview of the Bible. Beyond this though, the author shows his audience the supremacy of Jesus Christ and how the entire Bible relates to Him. Hebrews 11 traces a great deal of Old Testament history, but the rest of Hebrews shows how the Old Covenant's ritual and worship relate to Jesus. Relationship with God has always been by faith.

## BACKGROUND INFORMATION

The epistle (letter) to the Hebrews is included in a section of the New Testament typically referred to as the General Epistles. The General Epistles were not written to specific churches but rather to the Church in the general sense. Although grouped differently by various scholars, they usually include Hebrews, James, 1 & 2 Peter, 1, 2 & 3 John, and Jude. Based on the content of the letter, Hebrews was probably written to a more specifically Jewish Christian audience, but because no recipient is listed much about Hebrews remains a mystery.

## QUESTIONS of AUTHORSHIP and DATE

The real rub with this letter, however, comes not so much in regard to audience as to authorship. Why so? Because when the church fathers decided the canonicity of books that became parts of our Bible, one of the leading criteria was authorship. Hebrews is in the Bible largely because the church fathers thought Paul wrote it. Today, though, the prevailing view is that Paul did not write it. These scholars justify their view from both the style of writing and the fact that the author does not claim to have first-hand revelation. According to Hebrews 2:1-4, the author appears to have heard the message from those who heard it directly from the Lord. Paul always claimed to have first-hand information. Hebrews could be Paul's message without being his direct authorship. Some other names floated about in the discussion are Luke the physician, Apollos, Barnabas, and Priscilla either with or without Aquilla. There are tempting reasons to include each of these people in the discussion, but we need to end this with words from third-century theologian Origen: "But as to who actually wrote the Letter, God alone knows."

**ONE STEP FURTHER:**

**Get the Context**

If you're looking to take an extra step this week, read the book of Hebrews paying close attention to and recording every mention of Jesus and His superiority. I'll start you off:

Hebrews 1: Jesus is better than angels.

A BIG PICTURE
*Guide to the Bible*

Mystery also surrounds the date of Hebrews, again because the author gives us no direct information. Indirect information from the book, however, strongly suggests a date prior to AD 70. This date is critical in biblical history as it marks the destruction of Jerusalem and the temple under Titus (not Paul's Titus!). Because of extensive references to temple worship rituals it is hard to imagine its being written after AD 70 without any mention of the destruction.

## SO WHO WROTE HEBREWS?

Maybe only God knows who wrote Hebrews. But God *does know* and God sovereignly saw to it that it became a part of the Bible we use today.

## OBSERVE the TEXT of SCRIPTURE

**READ** Hebrews 11 and **MARK** every occurrence of the word *faith*. Watch for other repeated words and word groups.

### Hebrews 11

1   Now *faith* is the assurance of things *hoped for, the conviction of things not seen.*

2   For by it the men of old gained approval.

3   By *faith* we understand that the worlds were prepared by the word of God, so that what is seen was not made out of things which are visible.

4   By *faith* Abel offered to God a better sacrifice than Cain, through which he obtained the testimony that he was righteous, God testifying about his gifts, and through *faith*, though he is dead, he still speaks.

5   By *faith* Enoch was taken up so that he would not see death; AND HE WAS NOT FOUND BECAUSE GOD TOOK HIM UP; for he obtained the witness that before his being taken up he was pleasing to God.

6   And without *faith* it is impossible to please Him, for he who comes to God must believe that He is and that He is a rewarder of those who seek Him.

7   By *faith* Noah, being warned by God about things not yet seen, in reverence prepared an ark for the salvation of his household, by which he condemned the world, and became an heir of the righteousness which is according to *faith*.

8   By *faith* Abraham, when he was called, obeyed by going out to a place which he was to receive for an inheritance; and he went out, not knowing where he was going.

9   By *faith* he lived as an alien in the land of promise, as in a foreign land, dwelling in tents with Isaac and Jacob, fellow heirs of the same promise;

10  for he was looking for the city which has foundations, whose architect and builder is God.

11  By *faith* even Sarah herself received ability to conceive, even beyond the proper time of life, since she considered Him faithful who had promised.

---

## FYI:

**Think Civil War!**

In the next *FYI* box, I'm going to explain three dates you need to know in biblical history. Before that, though, I want to give you a little more information to help them stick.

In America we associate two directional words very strongly with the Civil War. . . the North and the South. In the history of Israel, these same directional terms carry tremendous weight.

Although Israel broke apart for different reasons than America did, the short-term result was the same—two separate countries. Under Saul, David, and Solomon, Israel was a United Kingdom, not unlike the United States prior to the Civil War. After that, they were a Divided Kingdom, the North and the South, again, not unlike the U.S. during the Civil War. The big differences? Although the North and South did fight from time to time in Israel, they coexisted as separate countries and never made up, both eventually being taken captive by foreign nations. More on this later!

12  Therefore there was born even of one man, and him as good as dead at that, as many descendants *AS THE STARS OF THE HEAVEN IN NUMBER, AND INNUMERABLE AS THE SAND WHICH IS BY THE SEASHORE.*

13  All these died in faith, without receiving the promises, but having seen them and having welcomed them from a distance, and having confessed that they were strangers and exiles on the earth.

14  For those who say such things make it clear that they are seeking a country of their own.

15  And indeed if they had been thinking of that country from which they went out, they would have had opportunity to return.

16  But as it is, they desire a better country, that is, a heavenly one. Therefore God is not ashamed to be called their God; for He has prepared a city for them.

17  By faith Abraham, when he was tested, offered up Isaac, and he who had received the promises was offering up his only begotten son;

18  it was he to whom it was said, *"IN ISAAC YOUR DESCENDANTS SHALL BE CALLED."*

19  He considered that God is able to raise people even from the dead, from which he also received him back as a type.

20  By faith Isaac blessed Jacob and Esau, even regarding things to come.

21  By faith Jacob, as he was dying, blessed each of the sons of Joseph, and worshiped, leaning on the top of his staff.

22  By faith Joseph, when he was dying, made mention of the exodus of the sons of Israel, and gave orders concerning his bones.

23  By faith Moses, when he was born, was hidden for three months by his parents, because they saw he was a beautiful child; and they were not afraid of the king's edict.

24  By faith Moses, when he had grown up, refused to be called the son of Pharaoh's daughter,

25  choosing rather to endure ill-treatment with the people of God than to enjoy the passing pleasures of sin,

26  considering the reproach of Christ greater riches than the treasures of Egypt; for he was looking to the reward.

27  By faith he left Egypt, not fearing the wrath of the king; for he endured, as seeing Him who is unseen.

28  By faith he kept the Passover and the sprinkling of the blood, so that he who destroyed the firstborn would not touch them.

29  By faith they passed through the Red Sea as though they were passing through dry land; and the Egyptians, when they attempted it, were drowned.

30  By faith the walls of Jericho fell down after they had been encircled for seven days.

31  By faith Rahab the harlot did not perish along with those who were disobedient, after she had welcomed the spies in peace.

**Three Dates You Need to Know**

There are three critical dates you need to know as you begin to build your knowledge of biblical history. I won't bait and switch or add more later. We'll review these throughout the course, so you can relax. Next time you see these dates in a sidebar, they will be a little more familiar and by the time we're done, they'll be old friends.

**722 BC** Assyria conquered the Northern Kingdom of Israel. Don't know much about Assyria? The capital is associated with a famous fish story.

**586 BC** Babylon captured Jerusalem, the capital of the Southern Kingdom, and deported its people.

**AD 70** Titus destroyed both the temple and Jerusalem. Hebrews was most likely written prior to this event.

**BC and AD**

BC = Before Christ. Those not so inclined to Jesus sometimes use BCE meaning Before the Common Era (i.e. Before Christ).

AD = *Anno Domini*, Latin for "In the year of our Lord."

A BIG PICTURE
Guide to the Bible

32  *And what more shall I say? For time will fail me if I tell of Gideon, Barak, Samson, Jephthah, of David and Samuel and the prophets,*

33  *who by faith conquered kingdoms, performed acts of righteousness, obtained promises, shut the mouths of lions,*

34  *quenched the power of fire, escaped the edge of the sword, from weakness were made strong, became mighty in war, put foreign armies to flight.*

35  *Women received* back *their dead by resurrection; and others were tortured, not accepting their release, so that they might obtain a better resurrection;*

36  *and others experienced mockings and scourgings, yes, also chains and imprisonment.*

37  *They were stoned, they were sawn in two, they were tempted, they were put to death with the sword; they went about in sheepskins, in goatskins, being destitute, afflicted, ill-treated*

38  *(men of whom the world was not worthy), wandering in deserts and mountains and caves and holes in the ground.*

39  *And all these, having gained approval through their faith, did not receive what was promised,*

40  *because God had provided something better for us, so that apart from us they would not be made perfect.*

## DISCUSS with your GROUP or PONDER on your own . . .

What is the main theme of this chapter?

What initial observations can you make from this read-through of Hebrews 11?

Based on a cursory look at Hebrews 11, what is faith? How does it act? What outcomes can it have?

What other words from the same Greek root as faith appear in verses 6 and 11?

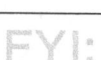

**FYI:**

**Sophisticated Greek**

The New Testament of the Bible was written in the common language of the day, Koine Greek, *koine* being the Greek word for common. Hebrews, while still written in the common language, ranks as a very sophisticated piece of writing. Its style is an evidence to some that Paul did not write it.

# DIGGING DEEPER
## What does it mean to gain God's approval?

Being able to read the Bible in English is a gift! We do, however, miss some of the nuances of the original languages if we don't set out to dig. If you're up for digging a little deeper this week, take some time investigating what *to gain God's approval* means. In the NASB we find this phrasing appearing in Hebrews 11:2 and 11:39, but the Greek word actually shows up four times in the first five verses. As you investigate, you'll also want to watch for the noun form of the word that frames Hebrews 11 showing up in Hebrews 10:28 and Hebrews 12:1.

What is the original word for *gained approval* in Hebrews 11:2? What part of speech is it?

What related word appears in Hebrews 10:28 and Hebrews 12:1? What part of speech is it?

How else are these words used in the book of Hebrews? In the rest of the New Testament?

According to the author of Hebrews, how does one gain God's approval?

Is there anything in your thinking or behavior that needs to be realigned based on this truth?

**FYI:**

**Key People and Events**

| Key People | Key Events |
| --- | --- |
| | Creation |
| Abel | |
| Enoch | |
| Noah | Flood |

**ONE STEP FURTHER:**

**It's Greek to me!**
Tired of relying on someone else to transliterate Greek words for you? Why not learn the Greek alphabet as you study Hebrews 11? If you studied *Sweeter than Chocolate: Psalm 119* and learned the Hebrew alphabet, you'll find Greek to be much easier, unless of course you're a native Hebrew speaker. As one of my favorite Greek profs always told his classes, "Greek is a very regular language!" Just think about it this week. Next week we take the plunge.

*Notes*

### For non-digital natives . . .

If you're using www.blueletterbible.org you can take the following steps:

1. Type in Hebrews 11:2. Change the version to NASB 95. Click the "Search" button.

2. When you arrive at the next screen, you will see a "Tools" button to the left of Hebrews 11:2.

   Click the "Tools" button to take you to the concordance at the Interlinear Tab.

3. When you arrive at the next screen, you will see the verse in chart form.

   Scroll down to find the phrase *gained approval*.

   Click on the Strong's number, in this case G3140, which is the link to the original word in Greek.

Clicking this number will bring up another screen that will give you a brief definition of the word as well as list every occurrence of the Greek word in the New Testament. Before running to the dictionary definition, scan places where this word is used in Scripture. Examine the general contexts where it is used.

## OBSERVE the TEXT of SCRIPTURE

**READ** Hebrews 11:1-7 and **MARK** the name of every person that occurs in the text. Also **MARK** any words that refer to *sight* or *seeing*.

## CREATION, ABEL, ENOCH, NOAH

### Hebrews 11:1-7

1 Now faith is the assurance of things hoped for, the conviction of things not seen.

2 For by it the men of old gained approval.

3 By faith we understand that the worlds were prepared by the word of God, so that what is seen was not made out of things which are visible.

4 By faith Abel offered to God a better sacrifice than Cain, through which he obtained the testimony that he was righteous, God testifying about his gifts, and through faith, though he is dead, he still speaks.

5 By faith Enoch was taken up so that he would not see death; AND HE WAS NOT FOUND BECAUSE GOD TOOK HIM UP; for he obtained the witness that before his being taken up he was pleasing to God.

6 And without faith it is impossible to please Him, for he who comes to God must believe that He is and that He is a rewarder of those who seek Him.

7 By faith Noah, being warned by God about things not yet seen, in reverence prepared an ark for the salvation of his household, by which he condemned the world, and became an heir of the righteousness which is according to faith.

---

## FYI:

### Who done it?

Who doesn't love a good mystery? Of course, mysteries related to the Bible can have unsettling effects if we're not careful about our thinking. Take Hebrews for instance. Among other reasons, this letter was considered for canonization based on Pauline authorship. But suppose Paul did not write Hebrews; what do we do with this?

Here's what *I* do: I trust that the God who was sovereign over the writing of Scripture was also sovereign over canonization, the process by which the books were recognized as inspired and strung together to make the Bible.

Now, who are some of the candidates for author besides Paul? Here they are in no particular order:

- Barnabas
- Apollos
- Priscilla, with or without Aquilla
- Luke
- Silas
- Clement of Rome

A BIG PICTURE
*Guide to the Bible*

## DISCUSS with your GROUP or PONDER on your own . . .

How does the author of Hebrews define faith?

What is the first event referred to in this chapter? How did the things we see come into being? What evidence does he give?

On what basis do we accept this as true?

While there is scientific evidence for creation and holes in the theory of evolution, we know that God created *ex nihilo* (Latin for "out of nothing") on the basis of revelation from God. Can you rest in this fact? Why or why not?

## ABEL

What does the text tell us about Abel's faith?

Remember, Hebrews 11 gives us summary versions. We're going to look a little closer at this account in Genesis 4:1-16. What's the rest of Cain and Abel's story?

---

### ONE STEP FURTHER:

**Make your case!**

If you're looking for a real challenge this week, spend some time investigating the possible authors of the book of Hebrews. Make your case for who you think wrote it and why!

---

### TRUE STORIES:

**Creation, Abel, Enoch, Noah**

Here's where you can find the main stories.

Creation:  Genesis 1–2

Abel:  Genesis 4

Enoch:  Genesis 5:18-24

Noah:  Genesis 6–10

To find other references to Abel, Enoch, and Noah try using the online concordance at www.blueletterbible.org. Just go to the web address and type in Abel, Enoch, or Noah as your search term! Amazing! It is always helpful to see the Bible's commentary on itself and a concordance is a great resource for doing this.

---

A BIG PICTURE
*Guide to the Bible*

Much has been made over the years about why Abel's offering was accepted and Cain's rejected. How does the author of Hebrews explain the acceptance of Abel's sacrifice?

How was Abel's sacrifice offered? (This is not a trick question. Go for the obvious answer!)

What tie does the author make between faith and righteousness? Can you think of other places in Scripture where you've seen this connection? If so, record them below.

## ENOCH

Okay, I probably shouldn't tip my hand here, but Enoch is one of my favorites in the Bible! So, if you're trying to do this lesson while at all groggy, go get a cup of coffee!

What does Hebrews tell us about Enoch?

Let's take a look at Enoch's story in Genesis 5:18-24 to find out how he pleased God. When you've read the account, record your findings.

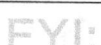

*Notes*

### FYI:

**Keep your brothers straight!**

Ever get Cain and Abel mixed up? I don't. It's not because I have a great memory; it's because I have a little, inaccurate poem my Dad was taught years ago in Sunday School.

*Cain killed Abel with the leg of a table.*

Remember, I told you it was inaccurate! I doubt there was a table leg involved, but the saying will help you keep from getting Cain and Abel mixed up!

What does Genesis 5:24 tell us about Enoch and God? How does Hebrews comment on them? What does the author identify "walked with God" with?

According to Hebrews 11:6, how can we please God? What two beliefs are necessary?

How do you try to please God? Take some time to think about this before answering. Further introspection may change your answer.

Is your "God-activity" more walking by faith or striving to please God in your own power? Explain.

Spend some time talking to God about this and asking Him to help you walk more and more by faith alone. Record additional thoughts below.

## NOAH

What does Hebrews 11 say about Noah?

---

**ONE STEP FURTHER:**

**Word Study:** *Pleasing*
If you have some extra time and/or energy this week, check out the following Greek words related to pleasing: *euaresteo / euarestos; aresko / arestos*. The first in each set of words is the verb, the second the noun. Record what you learn below.

---

*Notes*

# DIGGING DEEPER
## Looking at the *Sight* Words

Throughout Hebrews 11, the author uses a variety of *sight* words. If you have time this week, investigate these words and record your findings below. As you study, remember we are always doing this with an eye toward application!

How often are words related to sight used in this chapter and where?

According to Hebrews 11, how are faith and sight related?

What's hard to believe because you can't see it?

What actions are hard to take because of limited visibility?

How can this chapter inform your actions?

If you have time to read the entire account of Noah in Genesis 6 through 10, that's wonderful! If not, read at least Genesis 6:9-22. What did Noah and Enoch have in common?

Was Noah called righteous before building the ark or after and because of building the ark? Cite your reference.

We are inclined to think of Noah's big deal as ark building, and make no mistake; it was a big deal. But the bigger deal that led to the ark opportunity was that Noah, like Enoch, walked with God. God called him to build an ark as a result of faith that he already had. (See Genesis 7:1.)

Take some time to consider how you can more intentionally walk with God moment by moment. Record your thoughts below.

## @THE END OF THE DAY . . .

Based on what you have learned this week, how are you doing at living a life of faith?

One question we will return to throughout this study is how to walk when we can't see clearly. After all, "faith is the assurance of things hoped for, the conviction of things not seen." Is God calling you to walk when you can't see light all the way down the path? If so can you at least see where the path is lit for your next step? You may not have a clear answer now. If you don't, don't force one, but do keep the question in mind. Tell you what: I'll remind you of it as we continue on!

---

### FYI:

**Asking Questions of the Text**

The key to exegesis (that's the fancy word meaning *to draw out*) is questioning the text. The basic investigative questions Who? What? When? Where? Why? and How? will be your framework. Not every question can be addressed to every verse, and some verses require several variations of the same question. Although we're only focusing on one chapter of Hebrews, realize that we will not exhaust the questions that can be asked. Don't let that stop you from asking other questions and exploring further on your own. We will never run out of questions to ask and answers to glean from God's Word! And that's good news!! There will always be more to discover, apply, and live out!

---

As you close out your study this week, take some quiet time (30 minutes to an hour) to take a walk with God. When you finish, write down new thoughts God brought to your mind from His Word.

## ONE STEP FURTHER:

**The No-Guilt Pre-Test**

Can you remember back to grade school? The pre-test was always the one you took at the beginning of the week that didn't count. You took the test so you could see your progress. You'd start the week not knowing half the spelling words, but by Friday afternoon, you'd know considerably more, if not all of them. Take a few minutes and list to the best of your ability the major characters from the Bible you learned so far. Consider Hebrews 11 as your cheat sheet. Go!

## TAKE ACTION

What is one practical way you can apply the truth you've learned this week? See if you can compress your answer into one memorable word or phrase.

## Lesson Two
# Our Faithful God
# Empowers His People

*"Let us hold fast the confession of our hope without wavering,
for He who promised is faithful . . ."*
—Hebrews 10:23

*"By faith even Sarah herself received ability to conceive,
even beyond the proper time of life, since she considered
Him faithful who had promised."*
—Hebrews 11:11

The thought of walking into circumstances and situations we cannot see may stir feelings in our guts that run the gamut from mildly unsettling to absolutely terrifying! However, armed with faith in the promises of a faithful God we can walk not only with confidence but also with His power working through us. Are you tired of shuffling through life wondering what the future holds? As we'll see this week, Abraham didn't know what the future held, but he knew who held it. Here is a guy who by faith went out "not knowing where he was going"! Ever feel like you're not sure where you're going? Take heart! You're in good company.

And while we're talking about company, let me throw out another thought. Because it's so remote, it is easy for us to disengage from biblical history. It is easy to think, "That was then, this is now; that was their story and ours is another one altogether." It's easy to think of the Bible as old news, ancient stories, but in reality it is our family heritage. It is the story of who we are and so much more. While God's revealed truths, facts, and ethics ended with the book of Revelation, redemptive history did not.

The sovereign God who worked by faith in the lives of the men and women of Hebrews 11 is the same God who works in lives today. His people lived by faith then and His people live by faith now. We are part of a grand continuum, we are part of the rest of the story. Our story will never be recorded on the pages of Scripture, but we are nonetheless part of the line of faith and we are called to learn from the examples of those who have gone before. The God who warned Noah and called Abraham is the same God who calls you and me! Based on Hebrews 11, it is far less important to know where you're going than to know Who you're following! Sounds like an adventure to me!

## FOLLOW UP:

**How are you doing?**
That application we talked about at the end of the last lesson, how is it going?

## ONE STEP FURTHER:

**Thinking Ahead**
What are some important questions to ask regarding the background of the epistle to the Hebrews and its context within Scripture? What are good questions to ask along the way? What words should you look at more closely? Obviously, you'll find lots of questions throughout this workbook, but instead of just answering them start intentionally thinking for yourself. Always be thinking ahead. Anticipate questions, think about other relevant verses, consider other places in Scripture that might shed light on the passage in front of you. Always be thinking about where you would dig if all you had in front of you was the Bible. As you jot down questions, also be thinking about where you can find the answers.

## OBSERVE the TEXT of SCRIPTURE

**READ** Hebrews 11:8-22 and **MARK** every occurrence of *promise*. Continue to **MARK** references to *people* and *sight* words.

### Reading and Studying Tip: Begin with Prayer

You've probably heard it before but it is a phrase that bears repeating. Whenever you come to God's Book—to simply read or to study—first pray and ask His Spirit to be your Guide. The Bible is not an ordinary book. As Hebrews 4:12 says, "For the word of God is living and active and sharper than any two-edged sword, and piercing as far as the division of soul and spirit, of both joints and marrow, and able to judge the thoughts and intentions of the heart."

### Three Dates You Need to Know

I told you we'd be reviewing these dates. You'll have them down cold by the end of this study.

**722 BC** Israel, the Northern Kingdom, is conquered by Assyria. The famous capital of Assyria? Ninevah!

**586 BC** Jerusalem, the capital of the Southern Kingdom of Judah, falls to Babylon under the rule of Nebuchadnezzar.

**AD 70** Titus destroys the temple and city of Jerusalem. Hebrews was most likely written prior to this event.

### ABRAHAM through JOSEPH

*Hebrews 11:8-22*

8   *By faith Abraham, when he was called, obeyed by going out to a place which he was to receive for an inheritance; and he went out, not knowing where he was going.*

9   *By faith he lived as an alien in the land of promise, as in a foreign land, dwelling in tents with Isaac and Jacob, fellow heirs of the same promise;*

10  *for he was looking for the city which has foundations, whose architect and builder is God.*

11  *By faith even Sarah herself received ability to conceive, even beyond the proper time of life, since she considered Him faithful who had promised.*

12  *Therefore there was born even of one man, and him as good as dead at that, as many descendants AS THE STARS OF HEAVEN IN NUMBER, AND INNUMERABLE AS THE SAND WHICH IS BY THE SEASHORE.*

13  *All these died in faith, without receiving the promises, but having seen them and having welcomed them from a distance, and having confessed that they were strangers and exiles on the earth.*

14  *For those who say such things make it clear that they are seeking a country of their own.*

15  *And indeed if they had been thinking of that country from which they went out, they would have had opportunity to return.*

16  *But as it is, they desire a better country, that is, a heavenly one. Therefore God is not ashamed to be called their God; for He has prepared a city for them.*

17  *By faith Abraham, when he was tested, offered up Isaac, and he who had received the promises was offering up his only begotten son;*

18  *it was he to whom it was said, "IN ISAAC YOUR DESCENDANTS SHALL BE CALLED."*

19  *He considered that God is able to raise people even from the dead, from which he also received him back as a type.*

20  *By faith Isaac blessed Jacob and Esau, even regarding things to come.*

21  *By faith Jacob, as he was dying, blessed each of the sons of Joseph, and worshiped, leaning on the top of his staff.*

22  *By faith Joseph, when he was dying, made mention of the exodus of the sons of Israel, and gave orders concerning his bones.*

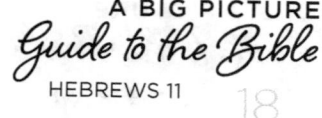

## DISCUSS with your GROUP or PONDER on your own . . .

What are your initial observations on the text?

What questions do you have?

What words or phrases would you like to focus on for further study?

Who are the main characters in this section of text and what did they do by faith?

What did you learn from marking promise? What was promised? Who promised it? Was the promise fulfilled?

Did you notice any more sight words? What did you learn from them?

Why were Abraham and Sarah able to persevere when they did not receive what was promised?

**ONE STEP FURTHER:**

**The Greek Alphabet**

Compared to English, Greek is a very regular language—at least that's what my professor always told us! While learning Greek grammar is certainly beyond the scope of this study, we'll take some time to learn the Greek alphabet. As you study the New Testament, being familiar with Greek will be helpful as you research words in the original language. For most English readers, learning the Greek alphabet is easier than Hebrew since the letters have a similar look. The fact that it reads left to right is an added bonus. Here are the first five letters to practice.

We're only going to work on the small letters. You'll catch on to the capitals if you start getting into any serious study of the language.

Take some time to write each letter several times.

| | |
|---|---|
| α | Alpha - "a" |
| β | Beta - "b" |
| γ | Gamma - "g" |
| δ | Delta - "d" |
| ε | Epsilon - short "e" |

1.

2.

3.

4.

5.

Have you ever known anyone with Abraham-type faith? If so, record a little bit about that person below. What specifically did you learn from this person that has helped you walk by faith?

## OBSERVE the TEXT of SCRIPTURE

**READ** Hebrews 11:8-12 and **MARK** all references to *land* and dwelling as a *foreigner* or *alien*.

### ABRAHAM and SARAH

*Hebrews 11:8-12*

8   By faith Abraham, when he was called, obeyed by going out to a place which he was to receive for an inheritance; and he went out, not knowing where he was going.

9   By faith he lived as an alien in the land of promise, as in a foreign land, dwelling in tents with Isaac and Jacob, fellow heirs of the same promise;

10   for he was looking for the city which has foundations, whose architect and builder is God.

11   By faith even Sarah herself received ability to conceive, even beyond the proper time of life, since she considered Him faithful who had promised.

12   Therefore there was born even of one man, and him as good as dead at that, as many descendants AS THE STARS OF HEAVEN IN NUMBER, AND INNUMERABLE AS THE SAND WHICH IS BY THE SEASHORE.

## DISCUSS with your GROUP or PONDER on your own . . .

Let's take a few minutes to look at Genesis 12:1-9. What did God call Abram to do? How old was he at the time?

We have several references to promise in Hebrews 11. What promises did God make in Genesis 12:1-9?

FYI:

**Abram and Abraham**

If you're new to Bible study, you may be wondering if there's a typo in the question to the right. After all, weren't we just talking about Abraham and now out of the blue the name Abram appears. Abraham's name started off as Abram. Along the way, however, God changed it to Abraham. God does that from time to time in the Bible. Sarai becoming Sarah and Jacob being renamed Israel are just a couple of other examples.

What does Abraham living as an alien mean? How is this similar to the way Christ's followers are to live?

Where else in the Bible does this concept show up?

How willing would you be to go out, not knowing where you were going?

Have you ever followed God going out, not knowing where you were going? How did it go?

Is God calling you to step out by faith to a place that you don't know? If so, how are you responding to Him?

How did Abraham benefit because of his hearing ears? How can we listen with the same heart toward obedience?

When did Abram set out? Why was he looking for the city?

Don't miss the fact that Abraham set out in response to God's call. He didn't well up zeal and courage (let alone interest) to travel to an unknown location (Hebrews 11:8); instead, a God his fathers had not served called him to step up and out. He didn't initiate the plan for his departure, God did; he simply responded obediently.

FYI:

**Do I have to mark the text?**
Of course not! Marking is simply a tool to help you make important words on the page stick out. Do you have to mark? No. Does it help? Yes.

If the thought of marking the text makes you break out in hives, don't do it. But if you can keep an open mind, give it a try! Before you know it you'll probably like the colored pencils!

A BIG PICTURE
*Guide to the Bible*

# DIGGING DEEPER
## Reading the Primary Source Material

Hebrews 11 will give you a jumpstart on the biblical story of faith and redemption, but nothing will substitute for reading the entire story yourself. Guess what, though! Just like Hebrews 11 is a high-leverage chapter, Genesis is a high-leverage book of the Bible. If you invest time in reading Genesis, you will find yourself with a great foundation for further Bible study. Genesis begins with an account of Creation and ends with the story of Joseph. So if you have time this week invest a bit of it in Genesis. This is a great text to read to kids or grandkids, too, if you're strapped for time. As you read, take some simple notes about the main characters of Genesis listed below:

Adam and Eve

Cain and Abel

Enoch

Noah

Abraham

Isaac

Jacob and Esau

Joseph and the twelve tribes

What is the most memorable truth you learned from the book of Genesis? How will you apply this truth in your life?

## ONE STEP FURTHER:

### Word Study: *Promise*

If you have some extra time this week, consider doing a word study on *promise*. What Greek word does the author of Hebrews use? What Hebrew words are used for promises in the Old Testament? What can we learn about the promises of God? Record your findings below.

## OBSERVE the TEXT of SCRIPTURE

**READ** Hebrews 11:13-16 and **MARK** any words that indicate what the people who died in faith were thinking about or seeking.

### *Hebrews 11:13-16*

13  *All these died in faith, without receiving the promises, but having seen them and having welcomed them from a distance, and having confessed that they were strangers and exiles on the earth.*

14  *For those who say such things make it clear that they are seeking a country of their own.*

15  *And indeed if they had been thinking of that country from which they went out, they would have had opportunity to return.*

16  *But as it is, they desire a better country, that is, a heavenly one. Therefore God is not ashamed to be called their God; for He has prepared a city for them.*

## DISCUSS with your GROUP or PONDER on your own . . .

Is God calling you to step out by faith to a place that you don't know? If so, how are you responding?

Where are your spiritual eyes fixed? Which direction are they looking?

Are you second-guessing what God has called you to do and looking backward? If so, why?

What thoughts do you consistently entertain? Are you viewing life through the windshield or in the rearview mirror?

## ONE STEP FURTHER:

**More on Marking**

As you mark the text, it is helpful to group similar words or types of words. I marked all *visual/sight* words in Hebrews 11 with a light blue pencil and distinguished different Greek roots with other marks. If this makes your head spin, just ignore it and move on. For those interested, here's what I did.

*blepo, apoblepo* - blue highlight with double box outline

*horao* - blue highlight with blue underline

*phaino, ekzeteo, ekdechomai* (all others) - simple blue highlight

This helps me see the extensive use of sight words while distinguishing the various Greek terms.

TRUE
STORIES:

### The Hagar Incident

If you're reading through Genesis in the *Digging Deeper* section, you'll pick this up on your way through. If not, consider reading the story of Hagar in Genesis 16.

Is it possible that in looking forward we can sometimes jump ahead of God? I think so . . . and I think if you asked Sarah, she'd agree. Record your thoughts below after reading and considering Genesis 16.

When we find ourselves "stuck" in life, sometimes a habit of looking back longingly is the problem. We see this in the Exodus generation. God was taking them to the promised land, but they insisted on grumbling and fixing their minds on foods they had in Egypt. Other times when we feel stuck, when we think we are "not receiving the promises," the problem's not the direction but rather our timetable. In these cases we can end up trying to make the promises happen (see sidebar True Stories: The Hagar Incident) instead of expectantly waiting for an all-powerful and sovereign God to act.

Have you ever been confused like Abraham and Sarah waiting for God to act? Did you push when you should have waited? What kind of results did you experience?

While Sarah especially did some pushing, the author of Hebrews commends her and others for looking in the right direction. They did not look back. Where had God brought them from? Where has God brought you from?

TRUE
STORIES:

### Looking Over Their Shoulders

The poster children for looking back were the Exodus generation of the children of Israel. You can read about them in Exodus and Numbers.

If you want to pinpoint specific instances of their backward looking ways, try searching on "Egypt" in a concordance. As you scan the entries, you'll quickly find the accounts so you can do some further reading if you have time.

Record your findings below.

Do you ever look back to your old ways? If so, how does it affect your walk with God?

What does the text specifically tell us they would have had if they were thinking about the country they went out from? What can we learn from this for our lives?

Has a backward-looking "What if?" become a long-term frustrating resident in your soul, diminishing if not paralyzing hope? If so, how can you evict it? What can you do? Who can you turn to?

## OBSERVE the TEXT of SCRIPTURE

**READ** Hebrews 11:17-22 and **MARK** every person the author mentions.

### ABRAHAM, ISAAC, JACOB, JOSEPH

*Hebrews 11:17-22*

17  *By faith Abraham, when he was tested, offered up Isaac, and he who had received the promises was offering up his only begotten son;*

18  *it was he to whom it was said, "IN ISAAC YOUR DESCENDANTS SHALL BE CALLED."*

19  *He considered that God is able to raise people even from the dead, from which he also received him back as a type.*

20  *By faith Isaac blessed Jacob and Esau, even regarding things to come.*

21  *By faith Jacob, as he was dying, blessed each of the sons of Joseph, and worshiped, leaning on the top of his staff.*

22  *By faith Joseph, when he was dying, made mention of the exodus of the sons of Israel, and gave orders concerning his bones.*

## DISCUSS with your GROUP or PONDER on your own . . .

Who are we told about in this section? Record their names below and how they are related if you know. If you don't, no worries, you will soon!

If the sacrifice of Isaac isn't one of the most disturbing stories ever on a surface read, I don't know what is! For little kids raised with bedtime stories from the Bible, well, let's just say this isn't the most sleep-inducing tale of the bunch. Now that you've already seen the Hebrews commentary on the account, take some time to read the primary source material from Genesis 22. How does the Hebrews passage help to explain the Genesis account?

Most of us either have or have had an Isaac, something so precious that the thought of sacrificing it, giving it up, losing it, is unbearable. What does God need to do to release your Isaac to Himself?

Do you believe God can be trusted with your Isaac? Knowing His character, will you choose to trust Him? Describe how you feel about this—why it's so hard, etc.

---

**FYI:**

**Do you have an Isaac to sacrifice?**

Years ago my husband and I participated in leadership training at our local church. We joined three other couples in a 40-week intensive process designed to help each of us clarify and live out God's call on our lives. While I learned much on the journey, the most important truth God stamped on my heart was that His call on my life needed to take *clear* priority over *any* positions I held at church or in ministry. This was not exactly new information to me, but I learned to apply it in a more practical way.

I found myself having to put good things down—ministries I loved—as I trusted God to use me fully wherever He chose. Was it a fun process? No way. Did I have doubts as I started putting things down and saying "No" to good causes? Yes. Was it worth it to focus wholeheartedly on God's call? Absolutely!

---

A BIG PICTURE
*Guide to the Bible*

# DIGGING DEEPER
## What did Abraham know and when did he know it?

## ONE STEP FURTHER:

### Waiting in the Life of Jesus

At the wedding of Cana, Jesus uttered these famous words: "Woman . . . My hour has not yet come." (John 2:4)

Let's think about this for a minute. Jesus comes to earth literally on a rescue mission and well into His adulthood He tells His mother Mary that His hour has not yet come. Although He knows He will live only into His early 30s, Jesus does not begin His public ministry until He is about 30 years old.

Let's face it, the type A's in the crowd would have been benchmarking (the nice way of saying odiously comparing) against other prophets: "Well, Samuel had quite the priestly ministry by age 12 and Josiah was king by age 8 . . ." Not Jesus. He may have wowed them in the temple at 12, but now He's living the quiet life, as far as they know, as a carpenter, until the beginning of His public ministry that happened *in God's time* and probably much later than either you or I would have scheduled it. Hmmm . . .

Type B's, you can just move on to the next assignment. Type A's, you may want to take some time to think about this and respond.

If you feel like digging this week, spend some time in the following texts that show the progressive revelation of God's promise to Abraham. The promise never changes, but along the way it becomes more and more specific. For each reference, note what is told about the promise, how old Abraham is at the time (if mentioned), and any other pertinent information.

Genesis 12:1

Genesis 13:14

Genesis 15:4

Genesis 17:16

How does the revelation of the promise become more specific over time?

Who is born in the interim?

Do you see how very specific the promise became over the years? By the time Abraham was asked to sacrifice Isaac, he had a minimum history with God of 35 years, probably more. He also knew that God would fulfill His promise through *this very son*. If God doesn't come through on this, Abraham will be sitting on a house of cards about to crumble. Of course at this point we know he built on the solid Rock!

**A BIG PICTURE**
*Guide to the Bible*
HEBREWS 11

## *Where We Are...*

Here is a simple recap to help get you up to speed on the story of redemption and fill in some of the gaps where Hebrews 11 hasn't connected the dots.

In the beginning **God** creates. **Adam** is the first man created, **Eve** the first woman. God creates them without sin and places them in the **Garden of Eden.** The serpent (later identified as Satan), however, quickly deceives them. Eve eats the forbidden fruit (from the tree of the knowledge of good and evil) first and gives it to her husband Adam. Through this act of sin death enters the world and God banishes Adam and Eve from their beautiful garden home.

Although **man rebels** against God, God immediately predicts the coming of a Savior who will crush the head of the serpent (Messianic Covenant). Jesus eventually fulfills this prophecy but in the meantime sin and death rule the day.

Eve bears Adam many children, the first two being **Cain** and **Abel.** Cain, resentful when God rejects his offering and accepts his brother Abel's, murders Abel. Sin gains speed and man continues downhill until God has simply had enough.

Saying He regrets making man, God tells **Noah** to build an ark in which he and his family will be saved from the coming destruction—a **worldwide flood.** Noah obeys and God saves him, his wife, his three sons, and their wives. After the Flood, God places a rainbow in the sky as a sign of His covenant with all living creatures that He will never again destroy the entire earth by water.

Noah's sons, **Japheth, Shem,** and **Ham** become fathers of all the nations. Over time the population of the world increases and people again veer off course. In pride they determine to build a **tower reaching to heaven** but during the construction God confuses their languages and thwarts their plans.

**Abraham,** originally named Abram, is the first major character on the scene after the Flood. Abram and his wife Sarai (whose name later changed to Sarah) live in the land of Ur. God tells Abram to leave his land and go to another one He will show him. **Abram trusts God** and packs his bags, taking his wife and household with him. Although God changes his name to Abraham and promises to make him a great nation, Abraham is within view of being triple-digit old with no blood-related heir in sight.

---

### FYI:

| Key People | Key Events |
|---|---|
| | Creation |
| Abel | |
| Enoch | |
| Noah | Flood |
| Abraham & Sarah | |
| Jacob (12 Tribes) | |
| Joseph | Egypt |

---

### FYI:

**Can God be trusted?**

Abraham wrestled with the same question that we face every day: Can God be trusted? We may not like to see it stated this bluntly, but when fears paralyze us, we're responding to circumstances like practical atheists.

Can God be trusted? The answer from God's Word is a resounding, "YES!"

---

A BIG PICTURE
*Guide to the Bible*

HEBREWS 11

What he does have, though, is a get-'er-done wife. After waiting "long enough" Sarah decides to act. She gives her handmaiden Hagar to Abraham as a second wife to scoot God's promise along. Not a good idea. Hagar bears Abraham a son named **Ishmael** but Sarah resents the outcome. Ironically the son of Sarah's plan is not the son of God's promise. He will be born later to Sarah.

**Isaac** is God's fulfilled promise to Abraham. Like his father, Isaac possesses a promise of descendants but has no children for the first 20 years of his marriage. But he prays for his wife Rebekah and God causes her to conceive twins, Esau and Jacob.

Although **Esau** is tough, he is spiritually dull. **Jacob** is instigating and conniving like his mother. The older twin Esau is tricked out of his birthright and blessing respectively by his younger brother and mother.

God chooses Jacob long before He changes his name to . . . **Israel!** Hence, the nation of Israel. Turns out deception runs in Jacob's family. After besting his brother twice, Jacob ends up on the other end of a bait-and-switch. Uncle Laban gives **Leah** to Jacob as a wife after he works seven years for her sister **Rachel.** Although Jacob sets out to marry only Rachel, he ends up with Rachel, Leah and each of their handmaidens. From Jacob and these four women descend the twelve tribes of Israel.

Jacob's most famous son is **Joseph.** Because he is also his father's favorite, his jealous brothers sell him into **Egyptian slavery.** Eventually God raises him up to be the equivalent of vice president of Egypt and reunites him with his family who **relocate to Egypt.**

After **Joseph dies,** everything is stable until a Pharaoh arises who "doesn't know" Joseph. He decides to enslave Joseph's family, now called the Hebrews, who have grown to great numbers in the land. The Hebrews remain **enslaved for 400 years** until the time of **Moses.**

To be continued . . .

# DIGGING DEEPER
## Doing a Word Study: Faith, part 1

Paul uses the word *love (agape)* nine times in the 13 verses of 1 Corinthians. *Spirit (pneuma)* occurs 21 times in the 38 verses of Romans 8, but *faith (pistis)* shows up a staggering 24 times (a round 25 if you include the verb form of the word) in Hebrews 11. Clearly *pistis* is the key word of Hebrews 11. Because this word is so important not only to this passage but also to the whole message of Scripture, your mission (should you choose to accept it) is to embark on a full study of it.

Here's where things may get a little confusing depending on your past experience in Bible study. Often we are led to believe that doing a word study involves looking up a word in a Bible dictionary or some other reference book, writing down what we read, and calling it a day. That is a way to learn how a word is used, but it is not doing a word study. It is copying the results of someone else's word study.

When we do any Bible study, the process should involve going to the primary source (the Bible) first, and secondary sources, second. In other words, we check word study books after we look for ourselves at how the particular word is used throughout the Bible.

Since faith is such a major word in the Bible, we are going to do a thorough study over the next several weeks.

To get started, this week simply use a concordance to find everywhere this word group appears in the New Testament, paying particular attention to the closest context first. The two words that we will focus our attention on are *pistis* (faith) and *pisteuo* (believe). You'll want to move from the immediate context outward. Record below what you notice about the usage of *pistis* and *pisteuo* in:

Hebrews 11

The rest of the book of Hebrews

In Luke and Acts

In Paul's epistles

**FYI:**

**Who wrote what to whom?**
Major authors in the New Testament include . . .

| | |
|---|---|
| Luke: | Gospel of Luke |
| | Acts |
| Paul: | Romans |
| | 1 and 2 Corinthians |
| | Galatians |
| | Ephesians |
| | Philippians |
| | Colossians |
| | 1 and 2 Thessalonians |
| | 1 and 2 Timothy |
| | Titus |
| | Philemon |
| John: | Gospel of John |
| | 1, 2 and 3 John |
| | Revelation |

## ONE STEP FURTHER:

**Practice the Timeline**

If you have a couple of minutes, make a quick list of everyone in the story of redemption you can remember without bringing on a migraine.

In John's writings

Elsewhere in the New Testament

Summarize what you learned this week from surveying the New Testament usage of *pistis* and *pisteuo.*

From what you have studied so far, how do these words compare to the English words *faith* and *believe?*

## @THE END OF THE DAY . . .

Spend some time quietly reflecting on where your mind typically dwells. Are you looking forward or backward? Does the direction you are looking indicate anything about your walk of faith? Explain.

## TAKE ACTION

What is your biggest backward-looking temptation? Is it a temptation to return to a former life you lived? Is it false guilt over forgiven sin? How can you combat this in your battle to look forward and fix your eyes on Jesus?

What is one practical way you will apply truth this week?

*Lesson Three*

# Are You Living a Bold and Fearless Life?

*"Now as they observed the confidence of Peter and John and understood that they were uneducated and untrained men, they were amazed, and began to recognize them as having been with Jesus."*
—*Acts 4:13*

*"By faith he [Moses] left Egypt, not fearing the wrath of the king; for he endured, as seeing Him who is unseen."*
—*Hebrews 11:27*

What does a bold and fearless life of faith imply? And how does walking confidently by faith differ from arrogantly pushing forward? We've already read about faith as the assurance of things hoped for, the conviction of things not seen. We know it is only by faith that we gain God's approval. We've also seen (above) that true faith sees the unseen and moves confidently toward it.

As we follow God, we need to discern the difference between moving forward in faith and acting out in pride or misplaced self-confidence. We must learn the moment-by-moment dance of hearing God's call and obeying as we submit to God's timing and wait for His power to be unleashed.

This week as we continue our study of God's sweet story we will look at Acts 7, another one of God's summary chapters that provides an interesting commentary on the life of Moses and gives additional depth to the Exodus account. Using Moses as our prime case study, we'll examine how to walk boldly by faith and avoid the pitfall of presumption.

FOLLOW UP:

**How are you doing?**
How did you apply the key truth you learned from last week's lesson?

A BIG PICTURE
*Guide to the Bible*

31    HEBREWS 11

## OBSERVE the TEXT of SCRIPTURE

**READ** Hebrews 11:23-29. As you do consider questions to ask and identify words for further study.

### Hebrews 11:23-29

23 By faith Moses, when he was born, was hidden for three months by his parents, because they saw he was a beautiful child; and they were not afraid of the king's edict.

24 By faith Moses, when he had grown up, refused to be called the son of Pharaoh's daughter,

25 choosing rather to endure ill-treatment with the people of God than to enjoy the passing pleasures of sin,

26 considering the reproach of Christ greater riches than the treasures of Egypt; for he was looking to the reward.

27 By faith he left Egypt, not fearing the wrath of the king; for he endured, as seeing Him who is unseen.

28 By faith he kept the Passover and the sprinkling of the blood, so that he who destroyed the firstborn would not touch them.

29 By faith they passed through the Red Sea as though they were passing through dry land; and the Egyptians, when they attempted it, were drowned.

## DISCUSS with your GROUP or PONDER on your own . . .

What are your initial observations on the text?

What questions do you have?

What words or phrases would you focus on for further study?

## FYI:

**Lengthening the Leash**

In your initial observation of the text, you'll notice I ask a lot of open-ended questions prompting you to ask your own questions.

I'm not doing this because my goal is to keep you doing my studies or anyone else's studies for the rest of your life. My goal is to equip you to study on your own without requiring anyone's assistance. If you find my studies helpful or if you like someone else's approach, that's fine. Just don't forget the goal is that you use studies because they are helpful, not because they are necessary.

How does this passage fit with what we have studied? Do you see similarities? Differences? Patterns? What life applications have you made so far?

## The CONTEXT of ACTS 7

Acts 7—another of the fabulous summary chapters of the Bible—contains a speech given by Stephen, the first Christian martyr, just prior to his death. Acts was written by Luke the physician who also authored the Gospel account bearing his name. Some also point to Luke as a possible author of the book of Hebrews but we need to remember that God's Word doesn't name the author, as it does for other books.

## OBSERVE the TEXT of SCRIPTURE

**READ** Acts 7:1-53. As you read, **MARK** the people who are mentioned and make note of anything new you learn about the Old Testament storyline.

### Acts 7

1   The high priest said, "Are these things so?"

2   And he said, "Hear me, brethren and fathers! The God of glory appeared to our father Abraham when he was in Mesopotamia, before he lived in Haran,

3   and said to him, 'LEAVE YOUR COUNTRY AND YOUR RELATIVES, AND COME INTO THE LAND THAT I WILL SHOW YOU.'

4   "Then he left the land of the Chaldeans and settled in Haran. From there, after his father died, God had him move to this country in which you are now living.

5   "But He gave him no inheritance in it, not even a foot of ground, and yet, even when he had no child, He promised that HE WOULD GIVE IT TO HIM AS A POSSESSION, AND TO HIS DESCENDANTS AFTER HIM.

6   "But God spoke to this effect, that his DESCENDANTS WOULD BE ALIENS IN A FOREIGN LAND, AND THAT THEY WOULD BE ENSLAVED AND MISTREATED FOR FOUR HUNDRED YEARS.

7   " 'AND WHATEVER NATION TO WHICH THEY WILL BE IN BONDAGE I MYSELF WILL JUDGE,' said God, 'AND AFTER THAT THEY WILL COME OUT AND SERVE ME IN THIS PLACE.'

8   "And He gave him the covenant of circumcision; and so Abraham became the father of Isaac, and circumcised him on the eighth day; and Isaac became the father of Jacob, and Jacob of the twelve patriarchs.

9   "The patriarchs became jealous of Joseph and sold him into Egypt. Yet God was with him,

10   and rescued him from all his afflictions, and granted him favor and wisdom in the sight of Pharaoh, king of Egypt, and he made him governor over Egypt and all his household.

11 "Now a famine came over all Egypt and Canaan, and great affliction with it, and our fathers could find no food.

12 "But when Jacob heard that there was grain in Egypt, he sent our fathers there *the first time.*

13 "On the second visit Joseph made himself known to his brothers, and Joseph's family was disclosed to Pharaoh.

14 "Then Joseph sent word and invited Jacob his father and all his relatives to come to him, seventy-five persons in all.

15 "And Jacob went down to Egypt and there he and our fathers died.

16 "From there *they were removed to Shechem and laid in the tomb which Abraham had purchased for a sum of money from the sons of Hamor in Shechem.*

17 "But as the time of the promise was approaching which God had assured to Abraham, the people increased and multiplied in Egypt,

18 until THERE AROSE ANOTHER KING OVER EGYPT WHO KNEW NOTHING ABOUT JOSEPH.

19 "It was he who took shrewd advantage of our race and mistreated our fathers so that they would expose their infants and they would not survive.

20 "It was at this time that Moses was born; and he was lovely in the sight of God, and he was nurtured three months in his father's home.

21 "And after he had been set outside, Pharaoh's daughter took him away and nurtured him as her own son.

22 "Moses was educated in all the learning of the Egyptians, and he was a man of power in words and deeds.

23 "But when he was approaching the age of forty, it entered his mind to visit his brethren, the sons of Israel.

24 "And when he saw one of them *being treated unjustly,* he defended him and took vengeance for the oppressed by striking down the Egyptian.

25 "And he supposed that his brethren understood that God was granting them deliverance through him, but they did not understand.

26 "On the following day he appeared to them as they were fighting together, and he tried to reconcile them in peace, saying, 'Men, you are brethren, why do you injure one another?'

27 "But the one who was injuring his neighbor pushed him away, saying, 'WHO MADE YOU A RULER AND JUDGE OVER US?

28 'YOU DO NOT MEAN TO KILL ME AS YOU KILLED THE EGYPTIAN YESTERDAY, DO YOU?'

29 "At this remark, MOSES FLED AND BECAME AN ALIEN IN THE LAND OF MIDIAN, where he became the father of two sons.

30 "After forty years had passed, AN ANGEL APPEARED TO HIM IN THE WILDERNESS OF MOUNT Sinai, IN THE FLAME OF A BURNING THORN BUSH.

31 "When Moses saw it, he marveled at the sight; and as he approached to look more closely, there came the voice of the Lord:

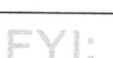

### Slow of speech and tongue?

In the Exodus account, Moses calls himself slow of speech, but Stephen refers to him as "a man of power in words and deeds." Ever wonder if Moses didn't have a correct estimate of himself? Ever find yourself saying something like, "I could never speak in public! God, you'll just have to find someone else." Perhaps Moses' speech problem was a problem in his own mind. We can't know for sure, but Acts certainly makes me wonder!

32 *'I AM THE GOD OF YOUR FATHERS, THE GOD OF ABRAHAM AND ISAAC AND JACOB.' Moses shook with fear and would not venture to look.*

33 "BUT THE LORD SAID TO HIM, 'TAKE OFF THE SANDALS FROM YOUR FEET, FOR THE PLACE ON WHICH YOU ARE STANDING IS HOLY GROUND.

34 'I HAVE CERTAINLY SEEN THE OPPRESSION OF MY PEOPLE IN EGYPT AND HAVE HEARD THEIR GROANS, AND I HAVE COME DOWN TO RESCUE THEM; COME NOW, AND I WILL SEND YOU TO EGYPT.'

35 "This Moses whom they disowned, saying, 'WHO MADE YOU A RULER AND A JUDGE?' is the one whom God sent to be *both* a ruler and a deliverer with the help of the angel who appeared to him in the thorn bush.

36 "This man led them out, performing wonders and signs in the land of Egypt and in the Red Sea and in the wilderness for forty years.

37 "This is the Moses who said to the sons of Israel, 'GOD WILL RAISE UP FOR YOU A PROPHET LIKE ME FROM YOUR BRETHREN.'

38 "This is the one who was in the congregation in the wilderness together with the angel who was speaking to him on Mount Sinai, and who was *with* our fathers; and he received living oracles to pass on to you.

39 "Our fathers were unwilling to be obedient to him, but repudiated him and in their hearts turned back to Egypt,

40 *SAYING TO AARON, 'MAKE FOR US GODS WHO WILL GO BEFORE US; FOR THIS MOSES WHO LED US OUT OF THE LAND OF EGYPT—WE DO NOT KNOW WHAT HAPPENED TO HIM.'*

41 "At that time they made a calf and brought a sacrifice to the idol, and were rejoicing in the works of their hands.

42 "But God turned away and delivered them up to serve the host of heaven; as it is written in the book of the prophets, 'IT WAS NOT TO ME THAT YOU OFFERED VICTIMS AND SACRIFICES FORTY YEARS IN THE WILDERNESS, WAS IT, O HOUSE OF ISRAEL?

43 'YOU ALSO TOOK ALONG THE TABERNACLE OF MOLOCH AND THE STAR OF THE GOD ROMPHA, THE IMAGES WHICH YOU MADE TO WORSHIP. I ALSO WILL REMOVE YOU BEYOND BABYLON.'

44 "Our fathers had the tabernacle of testimony in the wilderness, just as He who spoke to Moses directed *him* to make it according to the pattern which he had seen.

45 "And having received it in their turn, our fathers brought it in with Joshua upon dispossessing the nations whom God drove out before our fathers, until the time of David.

46 "David found favor in God's sight, and asked that he might find a dwelling place for the God of Jacob.

47 "But it was Solomon who built a house for Him.

48 "However, the Most High does not dwell in houses *made by* human *hands*; as the prophet says:

49 'HEAVEN IS MY THRONE, AND THE EARTH IS THE FOOTSTOOL OF MY FEET; WHAT KIND OF HOUSE WILL YOU BUILD FOR ME?' says the Lord, 'OR WHAT PLACE IS THERE FOR MY REPOSE?

**TRUE STORIES:**

**David and Solomon**

David makes the roster in Hebrews 11, Solomon does not. From the text of Acts we discover that David found favor in God's sight and Solomon had a building program. If you have some extra time this week, compare the life of David with that of his son Solomon.

Because there is so much biblical content about David, you may need to limit the scope of your study so you're not stuck in this sidebar all week.

Record your findings below.

*50* '*WAS IT NOT MY HAND WHICH MADE ALL THESE THINGS?*'

*51* "*You men who are stiff-necked and uncircumcised in heart and ears are always resisting the Holy Spirit; you are doing just as your fathers did.*

*52* "*Which one of the prophets did your fathers not persecute? They killed those who had previously announced the coming of the Righteous One, whose betrayers and murderers you have now become;*

*53* *you who received the law as ordained by angels, and yet did not keep it."*

## DISCUSS with your GROUP or PONDER on your own . . .

What are your initial observations on the text?

What questions do you have?

What words or phrases would you focus on for further study?

Who did Stephen speak about in his sermon?

Did you learn any details about these people that weren't included in Hebrews 11?

---

**FYI:**

**The Rest of the Story**

If you read the rest of the story about Stephen you'll find that the men who stoned him dropped their coats at the feet of the man who would eventually go on to write the majority of the New Testament, Saul . . . later known as Paul.

---

Re-read verse 52. What do the prophets of Acts 7:52 have in common with the people referred to in Hebrews 11:37-38?

## OBSERVE the TEXT of SCRIPTURE

**READ** Hebrews 11:23-29 and **MARK** every reference to *Moses* including pronouns. We are doing this to help identify every piece of information about Moses from this passage.

### Hebrews 11:23-29

23 *By faith Moses, when he was born, was hidden for three months by his parents, because they saw he was a beautiful child; and they were not afraid of the king's edict.*

24 *By faith Moses, when he had grown up, refused to be called the son of Pharaoh's daughter,*

25 *choosing rather to endure ill-treatment with the people of God than to enjoy the passing pleasures of sin,*

26 *considering the reproach of Christ greater riches than the treasures of Egypt; for he was looking to the reward.*

27 *By faith he left Egypt, not fearing the wrath of the king; for he endured, as seeing Him who is unseen.*

28 *By faith he kept the Passover and the sprinkling of the blood, so that he who destroyed the firstborn would not touch them.*

29 *By faith they passed through the Red Sea as though they were passing through dry land; and the Egyptians, when they attempted it, were drowned.*

## DISCUSS with your GROUP or PONDER on your own . . .

Using your marked text as a guide, compile a list of everything you learn about Moses.

---

### THINK ABOUT THIS:

**Questions that Make People Stop**

Let's face it, from time to time we find ourselves a little timid in our study, especially when we come to texts that appear inconsistent. Take Hebrews 11:27 and Exodus 2:14. The first verse says Moses wasn't afraid of the king's edict while the second says Moses was afraid when the matter of his killing of the Egyptian became known. Sometimes, instead of trusting that God has it all under control and boldly examining the text, we shrink away thinking that maybe, just maybe, God has missed a few things.

I've thought this from time to time over the course of my years, but I've come to tell you today that God's Word can be trusted. If you don't understand something, jump in and ask the question. God is big enough for you and your questions. Will we understand everything perfectly in this life? No, some things we have to accept as mystery, as beyond our ability to comprehend or empirically prove, but that does not mean they are not reasonable and cannot stand up to our questions.

Just my opinion here, but I think unasked questions feed doubt far more than honest questions brought to the light and pursued with a learner's heart.

God's not afraid of your questions. You don't have to be either!

What do we know about Moses' childhood?

How does he wind up as a "rebel" leader instead of a prince of Egypt?

In order to more fully answer this question, let's take a look at the primary account from Exodus as well as a closer look at Stephen's comments about Moses in Acts 7.

## OBSERVE the TEXT of SCRIPTURE

**READ** both Exodus 2:11-15 and Acts 7:22-29. As you do, **MARK** every reference to *Moses* including pronouns.

### *Exodus 2:11-15*

11  Now it came about in those days, when Moses had grown up, that he went out to his brethren and looked on their hard labors; and he saw an Egyptian beating a Hebrew, one of his brethren.

12  So he looked this way and that, and when he saw there was no one around, he struck down the Egyptian and hid him in the sand.

13  He went out the next day, and behold, two Hebrews were fighting with each other; and he said to the offender, "Why are you striking your companion?"

14  But he said, "Who made you a prince or a judge over us? Are you intending to kill me as you killed the Egyptian?" Then Moses was afraid and said, "Surely the matter has become known."

15  When Pharaoh heard of this matter, he tried to kill Moses. But Moses fled from the presence of Pharaoh and settled in the land of Midian, and he sat down by a well.

## Acts 7:22-29

22 *"Moses was educated in all the learning of the Egyptians, and he was a man of power in words and deeds.*

23 *"But when he was approaching the age of forty, it entered his mind to visit his brethren, the sons of Israel.*

24 *"And when he saw one of them being treated unjustly, he defended him and took vengeance for the oppressed by striking down the Egyptian.*

25 *"And he supposed that his brethren understood that God was granting them deliverance through him, but they did not understand.*

26 *"On the following day he appeared to them as they were fighting together, and he tried to reconcile them in peace, saying, 'Men, you are brethren, why do you injure one another?'*

27 *"But the one who was injuring his neighbor pushed him away, saying, 'WHO MADE YOU A RULER AND JUDGE OVER US?*

28 *'YOU DO NOT MEAN TO KILL ME AS YOU KILLED THE EGYPTIAN YESTERDAY, DO YOU?'*

29 *"At this remark, MOSES FLED AND BECAME AN ALIEN IN THE LAND OF MIDIAN, where he became the father of two sons."*

QUIZ:

**Write Your Letters**
If you've decided to take the plunge and learn the Greek alphabet, quiz yourself on the first five letters.

1.

2.

3.

4.

5.

## DISCUSS with your GROUP or PONDER on your own . . .

Compile another list of everything you learn about Moses from these texts.

What does Exodus tell us about Moses' incident with the Egyptian?

How old was Moses when he killed the Egyptian? Why did he do this?

How did this decision change the course of his life?

# DIGGING DEEPER
## So, let's ask it: *Was Moses afraid?*

If you have the time this week look at what Hebrews 11:27 and Exodus 2:14 have to say about Moses' fear or lack thereof.

What does Hebrews 11:27 say?

How does Exodus 2:14 compare?

Do these necessarily contradict? Why or why not? Is there any more to the story to consider?

What original language words are used for *afraid?* Does this information help? If so, in what way? If not, why not?

What did you learn from the greater contexts?

Finally, what do your commentaries say?

## ONE STEP FURTHER:

**The Greek Alphabet**

Your letters so far . . .

| α | Alpha - "a" |
| β | Beta - "b" |
| γ | Gamma - "g" |
| δ | Delta - "d" |
| ε | Epsilon - short "e" |
| ζ | Zeta - "z" |
| η | Eta - long "a" |
| θ | Theta - "th" |
| ι | Iota - "i" |
| κ | Kappa - "k" |

Have you ever made a poor decision you think will forever mark your life and leave you, practically speaking, unusable to God? What lesson can you learn from Moses?

Hebrews 11:25 tells us Moses chose to "endure ill-treatment with the people of God." What did this decision cost him?

Has choosing God ever cost you? Explain.

**TRUE STORIES:**

**Want to know more about Moses?**
For the full Moses account, head to the books of Exodus, Numbers, and Deuteronomy. To zero in on particular stories, try experimenting with an online concordance.

What did Moses do "by faith" according to Hebrews 11? (Look at the verbs in verses 24-29.)

Do you need to apply any of these verbs to your faith walk? Is there anything you need to refuse? Something you need to choose? Is there a place you must leave or situation you must endure? Explain.

As we bring our study to a close this week, we're going to look at one last Moses passage. In Numbers 20 we'll see Moses do something that will bring him devastating consequences.

## OBSERVE the TEXT of SCRIPTURE

**READ** Numbers 20:8-12 noting God's instruction, Moses' action, and the ensuing result.

### Numbers 20:8-12

8  *"Take the rod; and you and your brother Aaron assemble the congregation and speak to the rock before their eyes, that it may yield its water. You shall thus bring forth water for them out of the rock and let the congregation and their beasts drink."*

9  *So Moses took the rod from before the LORD, just as He had commanded him;*

10  *and Moses and Aaron gathered the assembly before the rock. And he said to them, "Listen now, you rebels; shall we bring forth water for you out of this rock?"*

11  *Then Moses lifted up his hand and struck the rock twice with his rod; and water came forth abundantly, and the congregation and their beasts drank.*

12  *But the LORD said to Moses and Aaron, "Because you have not believed Me, to treat Me as holy in the sight of the sons of Israel, therefore you shall not bring this assembly into the land which I have given them."*

## DISCUSS with your GROUP or PONDER on your own . . .

What did God tell Moses and Aaron to do in order to give water to the grumbling people?

What did Moses do instead?

What did the people do after Moses smote the rock?

FYI:

**The Importance of Cross References**

Scripture interprets Scripture. When an account in one part of the Bible leaves a gap and an ensuing question in the mind of the reader, often times (although not always) we'll find our question answered in another part of the Bible. Scripture truly does interpret Scripture.

# DIGGING DEEPER
## Doing a Word Study: Faith, part 2

If you decided to dig last week, you were up to your elbows in the Greek words for *faith (pistis)* and *believe (pisteuo)*. This week spend some time investigating how those concepts are used in the Old Testament of the Bible. What are the corresponding Hebrew words? Where are they used and how? Record your findings below.

*Faith* in the Old Testament -

To a casual observer, Moses got results. The water poured out and the people were happy. But he didn't do it God's way and it cost him entry in the promised land.

How often are you tempted to go about business your way instead of God's?

## ONE STEP FURTHER:

**The Greek Alphabet**
Greek students! Write the first ten letters of the Greek alphabet ten times each. Repetition is the key to learning a foreign language. Even if you don't pursue Greek language study, knowing the alphabet will help you more easily navigate scholarly resources.

1. α

2. β

3. γ

4. δ

5. ε

6. ζ

7. η

8. θ

9. ι

10. κ

Lesson Three: **Are You Living a Bold and Fearless Life?**

From what you know of Scripture, how does God's way contrast with man's?

What was so wrong with what Moses did? Do you see any connections with his pre-Midian ways? If so, explain. In each case, whose agenda was he seeking?

What can you learn and apply from this hard lesson of Moses?

## Where We Are . . .

Last week on our recap, we left the Hebrews in **Egypt** where they remained in bondage for 400 years.

Because the Hebrew population grows so rapidly, Pharaoh orderes **all male Hebrew babies killed.** He fears the slaves will turn against him if a foreign country invades. Moses' mother hide her newborn baby boy in a basket and sets it on the Nile River in an effort to save him. None other than Pharaoh's daughter draws the basket from the water and raises him as her own. As an adult, young Moses intervenes in a fight between an Egyptian and one of his Hebrew brothers, killing the Egyptian. He subsequently **flees Egypt** and becomes a shepherd in the **land of Midian** for forty years before God calls to him from a **burning bush** and sends him **back to Egypt** to lead the people **out of bondage.**

Although resistant at first, Moses obeys God and after a series of **ten plagues** and a celebration of the first **Passover** leads the Hebrews on their way to the **Promised Land.** Along the way God **parts the Red Sea,** feeds His people **manna,** and leads them with a cloud by day and a pillar of fire at night. Although the people arrive at the Promised Land quickly, ten of **twelve spies** sent into the land report a population of giants. Instead of trusting God's promise, the people shrink back in fear. God accordingly makes them wander in the wilderness for forty years before they finally enter the Promised Land.

Moses sees the Promised Land from afar but **Joshua** crosses the Jordan and brings the people into it.

To be continued . . .

## @THE END OF THE DAY . . .

How can we keep from sinning against God? By seeking His will and glory moment by moment and resting in His sovereignty over all. If we believe that God is sovereign, we can do what He has called us to do, leave the results in His hands, and rest in His timing.

Before you call it a day, take a walk with God and ask Him if you are lagging behind and looking back to the country from which you came. Ask Him if you are pushing forward with your own agenda. Ask Him how you can best walk the path of faith. Sometimes we don't know things because we don't ask.

## TAKE ACTION

What do you need to leave in God's hands today?

*Lesson Four*

# Review, Regroup, and Remember

*"All these died in faith, without receiving the promises, but having seen them and having welcomed them from a distance, and having confessed that they were strangers and exiles on the earth."*
—Hebrews 11:13

As we arrive at Lesson Four of our seven-lesson trek, we're approaching the halfway mark of our journey. You may be thoroughly engaged and raring to move forward by faith and if that is the case, great; I have a side quest to introduce to you in the next few pages!

I'm not so naive to think, though, that this walk through Hebrews 11 has been easy on everyone and that life has not reared its head and discouragement called at times. If this is you, if you're teetering between whelmed and overwhelmed or if you're already contemplating tapping out, Lesson Four is a time to slow down, do a simple review, and regroup for the second half.

So now more than ever, let the study flex to where you are. If you need to take a week off entirely and just read through Hebrews 11 once a day, do that. If you need a slower pace for a week, just do the first half of the lesson that will focus on reviewing the path we've already trodden. No guilt, no "I'll-do-it-laters." Just take one step at a time in the right direction. Some is always better than none.

If, however, you're ready for a little more this week, if you've been thinking, "Hey there is so much repetition in this chapter, I should be memorizing some of this . . . " do I have an opportunity for you!

## FOLLOW UP:

**How are you doing?**
That thing you decided to leave in God's hands last week—how is that going?

Just asking.

## REVIEW

Let's start with a simple review. As we begin today, read through the text we have covered so far and label each of the sections in a way that you will be able to recall. I suggest you use the least number of words needed to jar your memory. For example, if the term "Pre-Flood" makes you think the period that includes Creation, Abel and Enoch, simply term the first six verses "Pre-Flood." If you need more, include more but try to be as lean as possible. I've done the first one, you fill in the others. After each section record what you learned about faith in the section.

### Hebrews 11:1-29

PRE-FLOOD
.................................................................................................................

Creation, Abel, Enoch
.................................................................................................................

1   Now faith is the assurance of things *hoped for, the conviction of things not seen.*

2   *For by it the men of old gained approval.*

3   *By faith we understand that the worlds were prepared by the word of God, so that what is seen was not made out of things which are visible.*

4   *By faith Abel offered to God a better sacrifice than Cain, through which he obtained the testimony that he was righteous, God testifying about his gifts, and through faith, though he is dead, he still speaks.*

5   *By faith Enoch was taken up so that he would not see death; AND HE WAS NOT FOUND BECAUSE GOD TOOK HIM UP; for he obtained the witness that before his being taken up he was pleasing to God.*

6   *And without faith it is impossible to please* Him, *for he who comes to God must believe that He is and* that *He is a rewarder of those who seek Him.*

**Faith . . .**

.................................................................................................................

.................................................................................................................

7   *By faith Noah, being warned by God about things not yet seen, in reverence prepared an ark for the salvation of his household, by which he condemned the world, and became an heir of the righteousness which is according to faith.*

**Faith . . .**

### FYI:

**Antediluvian**

This is your fancy, Latin term for "pre-flood." When you start dipping your toes in scholarly commentaries, they often bust out big words for simple concepts. The prefix *ante*, simply means "before" and *diluvium* means "flood" (we get our English "deluge" from this).

.................................................................................................

.................................................................................................

8    *By faith Abraham, when he was called, obeyed by going out to a place which he was to receive for an inheritance; and he went out, not knowing where he was going.*

9    *By faith he lived as an alien in the land of promise, as in a foreign* land, *dwelling in tents with Isaac and Jacob, fellow heirs of the same promise;*

10   *for he was looking for the city which has foundations, whose architect and builder is God.*

11   *By faith even Sarah herself received ability to conceive, even beyond the proper time of life, since she considered Him faithful who had promised.*

12   *Therefore there was born even of one man, and him as good as dead at that,* as many descendants *AS THE STARS OF THE HEAVEN IN NUMBER, AND INNUMERABLE AS THE SAND WHICH IS BY THE SEASHORE.*

**Faith . . .**

**FYI:**

**Names to Know:**
***Torah* and *Pentateuch***

If you read a lot of commentaries, you'll start noticing words scholars like to use. Two words commonly used for the first five books of the Bible (Genesis, Exodus, Leviticus, Numbers, and Deuteronomy) are *Torah* and *Pentateuch*.

*Torah*, the Hebrew word for "law," is used to refer to Genesis through Deuteronomy. Although God commands things after these first five books, *Torah* nonetheless is a common designator for these books, also referred to as the Books of Moses or Book of the Law.

The other word associated with these books is *Pentateuch*. While *Torah* is a Jewish reference, *Pentateuch* is a Greek designation referring to the number of books contained in the grouping, *pente* being the Greek word for "five" and *teuchos* meaning tool, vessel, or book.

.................................................................................................

.................................................................................................

13   *All these died in faith, without receiving the promises, but having seen them and having welcomed them from a distance, and having confessed that they were strangers and exiles on the earth.*

14   *For those who say such things make it clear that they are seeking a country of their own.*

15   *And indeed if they had been thinking of that* country *from which they went out, they would have had opportunity to return.*

16   *But as it is, they desire a better* country, *that is, a heavenly one. Therefore God is not ashamed to be called their God; for He has prepared a city for them.*

**Faith . . .**

A BIG PICTURE
*Guide to the Bible*
49   HEBREWS 11

......................................................................................................................

......................................................................................................................

17  *By faith Abraham, when he was tested, offered up Isaac, and he who had received the promises was offering up his only begotten* son;

18  *it was he to whom it was said, "IN ISAAC YOUR DESCENDANTS SHALL BE CALLED."*

19  *He considered that God is able to raise people even from the dead, from which he also received him back as a type.*

20  *By faith Isaac blessed Jacob and Esau, even regarding things to come.*

21  *By faith Jacob, as he was dying, blessed each of the sons of Joseph, and worshiped, leaning on the top of his staff.*

22  *By faith Joseph, when he was dying, made mention of the exodus of the sons of Israel, and gave orders concerning his bones.*

**Faith . . .**

......................................................................................................................

......................................................................................................................

23  *By faith Moses, when he was born, was hidden for three months by his parents, because they saw he was a beautiful child; and they were not afraid of the king's edict.*

24  *By faith Moses, when he had grown up, refused to be called the son of Pharaoh's daughter,*

25  *choosing rather to endure ill-treatment with the people of God than to enjoy the passing pleasures of sin,*

26  *considering the reproach of Christ greater riches than the treasures of Egypt; for he was looking to the reward.*

27  *By faith he left Egypt, not fearing the wrath of the king; for he endured, as seeing Him who is unseen.*

28  *By faith he kept the Passover and the sprinkling of the blood, so that he who destroyed the firstborn would not touch them.*

29  *By faith they passed through the Red Sea as though they were passing through dry land; and the Egyptians, when they attempted it, were drowned.*

**Faith . . .**

## DISCUSS with your GROUP or PONDER on your own . . .

Briefly summarize what you've learned so far about Hebrews 11:1-29.

Now, take what you've written and condense it by one-half. Include memory prompts for the parts you leave out. (For example, words like FLOOD and EXODUS can prompt thoughts about what people were like before and after these events.)

Finally, as concisely as you can, summarize the story line of Hebrews 11:1-29.

What has been your biggest application point so far?

Do you have any striving behaviors in your life that are devoid of faith? If so, how are you addressing them?

Is God calling you to step out by faith in a direction you can't fully see? How?

---

QUIZ:

**Write Your Letters**
*(Open book if you need it!)*

Without looking, try writing the first ten letters of the Greek alphabet with their English equivalents.

1.

2.

3.

4.

5.

6.

7.

8.

9.

10.

---

**A BIG PICTURE**
*Guide to the Bible*

## REGROUP

If you've had enough, please take advantage of some time this week to slow down and think through what you've already learned. Summarize your takeaways so far along with one key truth from the text to meditate on this week.

## REMEMBER

Yes, now is the time that I invite you to memorize Hebrews 11!

I know. You have questions, the first of which is almost certainly: **Why?** Why memorize Hebrews 11 or anything else for that matter? While there's a biblical case to be made for memorizing in general, let me answer specifically for this chapter. Being highly patterned and for the most part chronological, Hebrews 11 almost begs us to memorize it. Doing so will help you learn the sequencing of the main storylines of the Bible and once learned, that knowledge will pull you forward with hints as you memorize and recall what you've learned.

Memorizing is work, there is no way around that fact, but hiding God's Word in our hearts pays dividends as we meditate regularly on His truth.

From the psalmist who says to the LORD, "Your word I have treasured in my heart, that I may not sin against You" (Psalm 119:11) to the apostle Paul who exhorts his readers to dwell on whatever is honorable, right, pure, lovely, of good repute, excellent and worthy of praise (Philippians 4:8), meditating on Scripture appears throughout the pages of the Bible as a core practice of the people of God.

## OBJECTIONS!

I know. You have objections. Let's consider a few of my favorites.

### But I'm too old!

You're not. The older you are, the longer it will likely take but that means you'll meditate more and more on the Scripture. You'll pay attention to what it actually says and means because you'll memorize by reasoning through it and not simply by rote as spongy-brained children do. It will take longer, but regardless of your age, you can do at least some . . . and some is better than none!

### But I've never been able to!

If you've never been able to memorize, my guess is that no one has ever given you actionable and effective strategies or you've underestimated the amount of time that memorizing takes those people who make it look easy. I'm pretty effective at memorizing, but it still takes hours and effort. I'm taking the time to share some of what has worked for me. What do you have to lose by trying?

## But I never remember what I've memorized!

While review and remembering is great, even when we forget some of it, the process of meditation on Scripture is what's most important. I don't remember everything that I've memorized, but I remember what I review and I'm still benefited by the time that I've spent meditating on Scripture that I can no longer quote word for word. Even when some of the words drop, the concepts and truth remain implanted.

## DIFFERENT APPROACHES

There is no right way to memorize. I use many approaches and strategies which reinforce one another, and I'm always on the lookout for more. Here are a few of my favorites.

### Listening.

Listen to the passage you're memorizing on an audio Bible . . . over and over again. Better yet, record yourself reading the passage so you can play your own heavily inflected reading on repeat. I use The Bible Memory App for this. I start off listening and before I know it, I'm joining and saying the words along with the recording.

### Writing.

Sometimes I type, but most often when I'm memorizing I hand write the verses or passages. A growing body of evidence suggests that handwriting actually helps us to remember content. Yes, handwriting takes more time than typing, but memorizing is not a race. Any memorizing recipe you find will have an extended bake time. Writing and re-writing helps.

### Thinking.

Perhaps it goes without saying, but perhaps not. When I was a child I memorized like a child—word for word for word—and often recalled content that I didn't understand. As an adult, much of the memorization process is thinking about what the text says and reasoning through what it means and how it fits together.

Part of the thinking process for me also involves watching for repetitions, terms of conclusion, any sort of patterns that I can leverage for recall. I'll point some of these out as we go along.

### Reciting.

As uncomfy as it is, reciting to another person helps in the memorizing process. Your listener can prompt you forward when you forget a word, give you encouragement to keep going, and provide needed accountability.

## ALL OF IT, REALLY?

Am I expecting you to memorize all of Hebrews 11? Not necessarily, but I do believe you can! If the whole 40 verses seems like too much, how about a verse? A few verses? How about listing the main characters and memorizing what they did by faith? Why not start small and give it a try? When you have some success, treat yourself to a prize and think about adding on!

> FYI:
>
> **Your Best Anti-Worry Tool**
>
> It has been said that worry is meditating on wrong things.
>
> Memorizing takes work and it takes space in your brain. You may need to purge some of what's going on between your ears to make room for it.
>
> Imagine for a minute your mind not having space to worry . . . Hmmmm . . .

A BIG PICTURE
*Guide to the Bible*

*Notes*

FYI:

**Facts to Help You Remember**

The phrase **"By faith"** begins 18 of the 40 verses in Hebrews 11.

In all there a total of 25 references to faith in this chapter.

Here are a few suggestions:

**One verse.**

Hebrews 11:1

Hebrews 11:6

Hebrews 11:8

**Section(s) of verses.**

Hebrews 11:1-6 (Definition of Faith; Abel through Enoch)

Hebrews 11:7-12 (Noah through Abraham)

Hebrews 11:13-16 (Summary of Faith)

Hebrews 11:17-22 (Abraham through Joseph)

Hebrews 11:23-29 (Moses)

Hebrews 11:30-32 (Jericho and Rahab)

Hebrews 11:33-38 (More of the Faithful)

Hebrews 11:39-40 (Approval Gained)

## WHERE TO START?

Start with time. Read. Re-read. Listen. Listen again.

Watch for repetitions and patterns. "By faith" shouts at us, other patterns whisper. Watch and listen. They often show up when you're elbow deep in the work. Don't panic if you're not noticing any right away.

Watch the sequence. Hebrews 11 is pretty chronological. When it inverts characters, note it and remember it.

**The biggest pattern . . .**

In telling the account of faith over the ages, our author follows a simple pattern:

"By faith" + subject (the who) + verb (the what he/she did)

The author adds other details to these basics, often including the outcome of the faith actions.

As you walk through Hebrews 11, the simple question to keep prompting you through the chapter is this: *Who comes next? What did he (or she!) do by faith?*

In order to start thinking through the patterns for yourself, take some time to list from Hebrews 11:1-31, the people, actions, and (when applicable) the outcomes in whatever detail you choose.

## Hebrews 11 "By Faith" Segments (1-31)

| Person | Action / State | Outcome |
|---|---|---|
| Abel | • **offered** a better sacrifice | • **obtained** testimony that he was righteous<br>• though dead still **speaks** |
| Enoch | • was pleasing to God | • obtained the witness that he was pleasing to God<br>• was taken up so that he would not see death |
| Noah | | |
| Abraham | | |

## Follow Repeating Words

While I can show you some of the basics for remembering Hebrews 11 in the graphics of the next few pages, you'll be able to remember so much more if you do some marking and follow some other repeating words and phrases watching how they flow through the text.

Here are the other words and word groupings that help me to remember this text. I've marked many of these; it may help you to do the same.

- **God.** How is God relating to the people of faith in this chapter?

- **Sight words.** Watch, pun intended, all the words referring to seeing—*seen/ not seen, visible, seeking, see*, etc.

- **Testimony / witness.** The same Greek word, *martureo*, refers to both Abel and Enoch. In verse 4 Abel "obtained the testimony" while verse 5 translates the same word to tell us that Enoch "obtained the witness." This Greek word also appears in verses 2 and 39 as "gained approval."

- **Dead / death.** References to death appear throughout the chapter. Watch for them and mark them. They'll provide bread crumbs to follow.

## Bits That Help Me Remember

- **Abel.** The verbs associated with Abel both start with "**o**" in English—**o**ffered and **o**btained. The alliteration of **s**till **s**peaks also helps me.

- **Enoch.** Whenever taken or took appears, it is linked with "up"—"taken up," "took him up," "being taken up." It's easy to drop an "up" unless you remember that it is part of every phrase.

**A BIG PICTURE**
*Guide to the Bible*
HEBREWS 11

## A NEXT STEP: Hebrews 11 Memory Prompts for Learning and Review

Over the next few pages, you'll find Hebrews 11 in a simple **Q&A format**. You can use this to help as you're memorizing or you can ask a friend to prompt you with review questions. The parenthetical italic questions will help to move you forward if you get stuck along the way. They will also help you to think through what is coming next in the text.

The **boldface** words help me recall the particular sections. They function as **prompts** for me. You'll notice in the first section they are typically the subject and the main verb—I'm focusing on *who* did *what* by faith. As the pattern begins to shift, my boldface prompt words shift more toward what is repeated in shorter sections.

My hope and prayer is that this simple structure will help you see the text in a slightly different and memorable way. You'll also find comments in the sidebars to give you some additional memory helps as you work through the text. Even if my process doesn't work for you, I hope it will prompt you to play with different and creative ways to remember.

*What is faith?*

**1** Now **faith is**
1. the **assurance** of things hoped for, *(what else?)*
2. the **conviction** of things not seen.

*What result did faith have in the past?*

**2** For by it the **men of old** • **gained approval.**

*What do we understand by faith?*

**3** By faith **we**
- **understand** that the worlds were prepared by the word of God, *(so what?)*
- so that what is seen was not made out of things which are visible.

*What did Abel do by faith?*

**4** By faith **Abel**
- **offered** to God a better sacrifice than Cain *(what did he obtain through this?)*
- through which he **obtained the testimony** that he was righteous, *(who testified?)*
- God testifying about his gifts, and *(what is the current result?)*
- through faith though he is dead, he **still speaks.**

*What did Enoch do by faith?*

**5** By faith **Enoch**
- was taken up so that he would not see death; *(Why was he not found?)*
- AND HE WAS NOT FOUND BECAUSE GOD TOOK HIM UP *(why was this?)*
- for he **obtained the witness** that before his being taken up he was pleasing to God.

*What lack makes it impossible to please God?*

**6**  And **without faith** it is **impossible** to please Him, *(why?)*

for he who comes to God **must believe:** *(what?)*

- **that He is** and
- **that He is a rewarder** of those who seek Him.

*What did Noah do by faith and why?*

**7**  By faith **Noah**

- being warned by God about things not yet seen
- in reverence **prepared an ark** *(why?)* for the salvation of his household, *(what other effects did it have?)*
- by which he **condemned the world,** and *(what else?)*
- **became an heir** of the righteousness which is according to faith.

*What did Abraham do by faith and when?*

**8**  By faith **Abraham**

- when he was called,
- **obeyed** *(how?)* **by going out** to a place which he was to receive for an inheritance; and
- he **went out,** *(how?)* not knowing where he was going.

**9**  By faith **he**

- **lived as an alien** in the land of promise, *(how?)* as in a foreign land
- **dwelling in tents** with Isaac and Jacob, *(who?)* fellow heirs of the same promise; *(why?)*

**10**

- for he **was looking** for the city *(which city?)*
- which has its foundations, whose
  1. **architect** and
  2. **builder** is God.

*What did even Sarah do by faith and when?*

**11**  By faith even **Sarah** herself

- **received** ability to conceive, *(when?)* even beyond the proper time of life, *(why?)*
- since she **considered** Him faithful who had promised.

---

### Patterns Obvious and Otherwise

We've already talked about the main pattern in this chapter: by faith + subject + action. The longer you sit with these verses, the more patterns you'll see. As you start noticing other patterns and ways of remembering content or word sequences, mark them down! I'm sharing with you just a few of mine. Those you discover on your own will almost certainly be easier for you to remember! Mark this text, start with a fresh text, use colored pencils . . . or don't. The more time you spend with the text, the more potential ways you'll see to remember and recall what is there!! You may not believe me yet, but it becomes more and more fun the longer you do it.

### Pattern Breaks and Sub-Patterns

When patterns break, be aware and use that as a memory hook of its own. We're told about Enoch's "being taken up" prior to hearing about him having "obtained the witness."

Both Noah and Abraham also break the strict "By faith + person + action" pattern with Noah's faith action being prompted by God's warning and Abraham's by God's call.

A BIG PICTURE
*Guide to the Bible*

*Notes*

## Contrasts
Since the main pattern has shifted in verse 12, I'm keying in on a key contrast—the growth from "one man" to "many descendants" to help me remember.

## Writing to See Patterns
Without writing this out or reading it aloud, it's easy to miss the rhythm in the participles:
- **having** seen,
- **having** welcomed,
- **having** confessed.

Those who died in faith had not receive the promises (yet!), but from a distance they saw, welcomed, and confessed.

## The Better Country
In the summary verses of 14–16, I'm focusing on "the country" to pull me forward through the verses. What country are they seeking and desiring? What country are they not thinking about? These verses aren't as simple to remember as the "by faith" section, but by the time you get to them, you'll be better at memorizing.

---

*What was the big outcome of this?*

**12** Therefore
- there was born even of **one man**, *(what else?)* and him as good as dead at that
- as many **descendants**
  1. AS THE STARS OF THE HEAVEN IN NUMBER, AND
  2. AS INNUMERABLE AS THE SAND WHICH IS BY THE SEASHORE.

*What were these people like? What did they receive and not receive?*

**13** All these died in faith
- without receiving the promises, but
- **having seen** them and
- **having welcomed** them from a distance, and
- **having confessed** that they were
  1. strangers and
  2. exiles on the earth.

*What do people of faith make clear?*

**14** For those who say such things make it clear that
- they are **seeking a country** of their own.

*What do we learn about their thinking?*

**15** And indeed if they
- had been **thinking of that country** from which they went out,
- they would have had opportunity to return.

*What do we learn about their desire?*

**16** But as it is, they
- **desire a better country,**
- that is, a heavenly one.

*What does the text tell us about God?*

Therefore
- God is **not ashamed** to be called their God;
- for He **has prepared** a city for them.

*Notes*

*What else did Abraham do by faith and when?*

**17** By faith **Abraham**, 
- when he was **tested**
- **offered up** Isaac, and

**he** who had received the promises 
- **was offering up** his only begotten son;

**18**
- it was he to whom it was said,
- "IN ISAAC YOUR DESCENDANTS SHALL BE CALLED."

**19** **He** [Abraham]
- **considered** that God is able to raise people even from the dead,
  - from which he also received him back as a type.

*What did Isaac do by faith?*

**20** By faith **Isaac**
- **blessed** Jacob and Esau,
- even regarding things to come.

*What did Jacob do by faith and when?*

**21** By faith **Jacob**
- as he was dying
- **blessed** each of the sons of Joseph, and
- **worshiped,** leaning on the top of his staff.

*What did Joseph do by faith and when?*

**22** By faith **Joseph**
- when he was dying
- **made mention** of the exodus of the sons of Israel, and
- **gave orders** concerning his bones.

*What did Moses do by faith?*

**23** By faith **Moses**
- when he **was born,**
- **was hidden** for three months by his parents

[Moses' parents]
- because **they saw** he was a beautiful child; and
- **they were not afraid** of the king's edict.

---

### Watch the Timing!

We were told back in verse 8 what Abraham did when he was called, now we find out what he did when he was tested. We can also follow the "when" train with Jacob (as he was dying), Joseph (when he was dying), and Moses (when he was born; when he had grown up). I couldn't help myself, so I've circled them on this page!

---

### A Simple Scaffold

I often use simple mnemonic devices to help with my initial memorization that will fall away once I have actually learned the verse. Let me show you one in verses 21-22.

The "dying" phrases of Jacob and Joseph differ slightly but I remind myself that they are in alphabetical order:

"**a**s he was dying" (Jacob, verse 21)

"**w**hen he was dying" (Joseph verse 22)

If this seems stupid to you, don't give it a second thought. If it makes sense, watch for other instances that can help you!

---

A BIG PICTURE
*Guide to the Bible*

*Notes*

*What else?*

24 By faith **Moses** (• when) he **had grown up,**

- **refused** to be called the son of Pharaoh's daughter,

25
- **choosing**
  - rather **to endure** ill-treatment with the people of God
  - than **to enjoy** the passing pleasures of sin,

26
- **considering**
  - the **reproach** of Christ greater riches
  - than the **treasures** of Egypt;

for **he**
- **was looking** to the reward.

---

**Greater Than**

Christ's reproach > Egypt's treasures

---

*What else did Moses do by faith?*

27 By faith **he**
- **left** Egypt, not fearing the wrath of the king;

for **he**
- **endured,** as seeing Him who is unseen.

*What else did Moses do by faith?*

28 By faith **he**
- **kept** the Passover and the sprinkling of the blood,
- **so that** he who destroyed the firstborn would not touch them.

---

**More Contrasts**

In verse 29 watch the contrast between:

the **Israelites** who **passed through**

and

the **Egyptians** who **were drowned.**

---

*What did the Israelites do by faith?*

29 By faith **they** [the Exodus generation]
- **passed through** the Red Sea *(how?)*
- as though they were passing through dry land; *(only them?)*
- and the **Egyptians,**
- when they attempted it, **were drowned.**

---

**Tiny Patterns**

Even as I'm writing this out for you, I'm seeing memory hooks as a write. Notice the "after"s in verses 30 and 31.

Jericho's walls fell down **after they** . . .

Rahab did not perish . . . **after she** . . .

Think of this as scaffolding that will come out after the building is complete.

---

*What happened at Jericho?*

30 By faith the walls of Jericho
- **fell down**
- after they had been encircled for seven days.

*What did Rahab do by faith?*

31 By faith **Rahab** the harlot
- **did not perish** along with those who were disobedient
- after she had **welcomed** the spies in peace.

A BIG PICTURE
*Guide to the Bible*
HEBREWS 11   60

*Is there more?*

**32** And what more shall I say? For time will fail me if I tell of

**Gideon, Barak,**

**Samson, Jephthah**, of

**David** and **Samuel** and

the **prophets**

**Reverse-Order Pairs**
I've memorized these as three pairs of two, each of which is listed in reverse order of their appearance in Scripture.

*What did they do?*

**33** **who** by faith

1. conquered kingdoms
2. performed acts of righteousness
3. obtained promises
4. shut the mouths of lions

**The Highs**
I remember that there are nine happier outcomes. Pick out the word in each one that works best for you as your anchor word and leverage the contrasts (weakness/strong) and letter repetitions (escaped the edge; foreign armies to flight) to help you remember.

*What else?*

**34**

5. quenched the power of fire
6. escaped the edge of the sword
7. from weakness were made strong
8. became mighty in war
9. put foreign armies to flight.

*Were all the outcomes good?*

**35** **Women**

and **others**

- received back their dead **by resurrection;**
- were **tortured**, not accepting their release
- so that they might obtain a **better resurrection**

**Temporal versus Eternal**
Resurrection here or resurrection there!

*What hard things happened?*

**36** and **others**
**experienced**

1. **mockings** and **scourgings**, yes also (2 persecutions)
2. **chains** and **imprisonment**. (2 confinements)

**37** **They**

**they**

**they**

**they**

3. were **stoned**,
4. were **sawn** in two,
5. were put to death with the **sword**;
6. went about in **sheepskins**, in **goatskins** (2 skins)
7. being **destitute**, **afflicted**, **ill-treated** (3 conditions)

**The Lows**
Contrasting the happy endings are a series of sobering outcomes. I'm grouping these into nine entries. If you want to try and remember 18 facts, you can do that. I prefer to group the second batch to parallel the first set.

**38**

8. (men of whom the world was not worthy),
9. wandering in **deserts** and **mountains** and **caves** and **holes** in the ground. (4 locations)

**39**   And all these,
- having **gained approval** through their faith,
- **did not receive** what was promised

**40**
- because God had provided **something better** for us,
- so that **apart from us they would not be made perfect**.

## @THE END OF THE DAY...

Perhaps an action you can take by faith this week is to memorize and meditate on God's Word even though it may seem like a daunting task. Remember everything that the people of Hebrews 11 did, they did by faith!

## TAKE ACTION

What, if anything, will you commit to memorizing? Who will you ask to help you?

# Hope for the Rest of Us— God Works in Flawed People

*"By faith Rahab the harlot did not perish along with those who were disobedient, after she had welcomed the spies in peace."*
—Hebrews 11:31

Just the title "The Faith Chapter" that is so often attributed to Hebrews 11 can be very intimidating. If that's not enough, looking at the lives of Noah, Abraham, and Moses who in spite of their flaws walked so closely with God verges on overwhelming. After all who are you and I to consider our faith worthy of mention in the same breath as theirs? Faith, however, has far more to do with objects than with the subjects who believe. Noah, Abraham, and Moses aren't commended for unanchored faith of their own making; they testify to a God who is and who rewards those who seek Him. Their faith is not in their actions, their feeble attempts at goodness, but in a God who for His own reasons bends down to save and work through flawed people.

If you've been feeling a little "less than" as we've been working our way through these giants of the faith, if you've been feeling more flawed and less worthy then take heart! This week the author of Hebrews will lead us on an adventure into the biblical time of Joshua and Judges where we will see without doubt that our holy God has a way of working in the lives of flawed people—sometimes in spite of themselves.

## FOLLOW UP:

**How are you doing?**
Have you been working on memorizing a verse from Hebrews 11?

If so, what has been most encouraging in the process?

## FYI:

**Who is where in the Bible?**
Genesis: Creation, Abel, Enoch, Noah, Abraham, Isaac, Jacob, Joseph

Exodus-Deuteronomy: Moses and the wilderness generation of Israel

Joshua: Rahab

Judges: Barak, Gideon, Jephthah, Samson

## OBSERVE the TEXT of SCRIPTURE

While the author of Hebrews invests 22 verses from the book of Genesis alone, he picks up serious speed as he nears the three-quarter mark in his treatise. Verses 30 and 31 refer to events in the book of Joshua, verse 32 begins with men from the time of Judges. Again, label each section to help you recall it and then record what you learned about faith.

**READ** Hebrews 11:30-34. **CIRCLE** every person who is mentioned by name and **UNDERLINE** every action attributed to the unnamed people of faith.

### Hebrews 11:30-31

..........................................................................................................................

..........................................................................................................................

30  *By faith the walls of Jericho fell down after they had been encircled for seven days.*

31  *By faith Rahab the harlot did not perish along with those who were disobedient, after she had welcomed the spies in peace.*

**Faith . . .**

### Hebrews 11:32-34

..........................................................................................................................

..........................................................................................................................

32  *And what more shall I say? For time will fail me if I tell of Gideon, Barak, Samson, Jephthah, of David and Samuel and the prophets,*

33  *who by faith conquered kingdoms, performed acts of righteousness, obtained promises, shut the mouths of lions,*

34  *quenched the power of fire, escaped the edge of the sword, from weakness were made strong, became mighty in war, put foreign armies to flight.*

**Faith . . .**

## DISCUSS with your GROUP or PONDER on your own . . .

What do you already know about: Jericho? Rahab? The Spies? Gideon? Barak? Samson? Jephthah?

---

### ONE STEP FURTHER:

**The Greek Alphabet**

Your letters so far . . .

| | |
|---|---|
| α | Alpha - "a" |
| β | Beta - "b" |
| γ | Gamma - "g" |
| δ | Delta - "d" |
| ε | Epsilon - short "e" |
| ζ | Zeta - "z" |
| η | Eta - long "a" |
| θ | Theta - "th" |
| ι | Iota - "i" |
| κ | Kappa - "k" |
| λ | Lamda - "l" |
| μ | Mu - "m" |
| ν | Nu - "n" |
| ξ | Xi - "x" |
| ο | Omicron - short "o" |
| π | Pi - "p" (pronounced like our letter "p") |
| ρ | Rho - "r" |

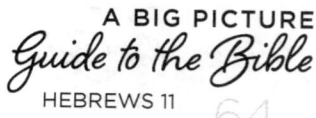

How can you find more information about these people? Where will you start? Where can you find secondary texts? What other tools can you use to find out more about the people and accounts referred to here?

## OBSERVE the TEXT of SCRIPTURE

The first event mentioned in this section is the fall of the walls of Jericho, and the first person of faith is Rahab.

**READ** Joshua 6, the account of the fall of Jericho. Use a Bible you have on hand or read online at www.blueletterbible.com.

## DISCUSS with your GROUP or PONDER on your own . . .

What do we know about Jericho from the first few verses? Why was it shut up so tightly?

Why does the wall event at Jericho make the faith chapter?

What specific "battle" instructions did God give the Israelites? How do the people respond?

What happens when Joshua and the people respond in faith?

Before moving on, spend some time asking God if there are any cities that you have been planning on storming that He would have you march around instead.

**FYI:**

**Joshua and Judges**

The books of Joshua and Judges sit between Moses and the kings of Israel. Joshua is a book of overwhelming victory, Judges a book of profound defeat.

The book of Joshua records events related to the children of Israel entering and taking possession of the promised land under Joshua, the man God placed in leadership upon the death of His servant Moses.

After Joshua and the elders who followed him died, the people's hearts wandered. This period of ruling judges was marked by cycles of sin. Israel sinned, God brought foreign powers to subdue them, they cried out for deliverance, God sent deliverers (judges), they obeyed until the judge died, and then the cycle began again. The book of Ruth also takes place against this backdrop. During the time of the judges, we read "every man did what was right in his own eyes."

## OBSERVE the TEXT of SCRIPTURE

Now that we've seen the fall of Jericho for ourselves, let's step back in the text to Joshua 2 and the account of Rahab. This one we'll look at in the workbook, along with the comment on Rahab from the final portion of Joshua 6.

**READ** Joshua 2 and Joshua 6:17-27. As you do, **CIRCLE** every reference to *Rahab* and her family and **UNDERLINE** every reference to *Jericho* and its people.

### Joshua 2

1   Then Joshua the son of Nun sent two men as spies secretly from Shittim, saying, "Go, view the land, especially Jericho." So they went and came into the house of a harlot whose name was Rahab, and lodged there.

2   It was told the king of Jericho, saying, "Behold, men from the sons of Israel have come here tonight to search out the land."

3   And the king of Jericho sent word to Rahab, saying, "Bring out the men who have come to you, who have entered your house, for they have come to search out all the land."

4   But the woman had taken the two men and hidden them, and she said, "Yes, the men came to me, but I did not know where they were from.

5   "It came about when it was time to shut the gate at dark, that the men went out; I do not know where the men went. Pursue them quickly, for you will overtake them."

6   But she had brought them up to the roof and hidden them in the stalks of flax which she had laid in order on the roof.

7   So the men pursued them on the road to the Jordan to the fords; and as soon as those who were pursuing them had gone out, they shut the gate.

8   Now before they lay down, she came up to them on the roof,

9   and said to the men, "I know that the LORD has given you the land, and that the terror of you has fallen on us, and that all the inhabitants of the land have melted away before you.

10  "For we have heard how the LORD dried up the water of the Red Sea before you when you came out of Egypt, and what you did to the two kings of the Amorites who were beyond the Jordan, to Sihon and Og, whom you utterly destroyed.

11  "When we heard it, our hearts melted and no courage remained in any man any longer because of you; for the LORD your God, He is God in heaven above and on earth beneath.

12  "Now therefore, please swear to me by the LORD, since I have dealt kindly with you, that you also will deal kindly with my father's household, and give me a pledge of truth,

13  and spare my father and my mother and my brothers and my sisters, with all who belong to them, and deliver our lives from death."

14  So the men said to her, "Our life for yours if you do not tell this business of ours; and it shall come about when the LORD gives us the land that we will deal kindly and faithfully with you."

FYI:

**Will the Greek alphabet actually help me?**

Years ago my son and I spent a college-visit day at Moody Bible Institute in Chicago. We attended a Romans class in the morning and a Hermeneutics class in the evening. Know what they were learning in Hermeneutics? The Greek alphabet. Know why? So they can better use original language study tools. It's not necessary to learn, but it's extremely helpful.

15   Then she let them down by a rope through the window, for her house was on the city wall, so that she was living on the wall.

16   She said to them, "Go to the hill country, so that the pursuers will not happen upon you, and hide yourselves there for three days until the pursuers return. Then afterward you may go on your way."

17   The men said to her, "We shall be free from this oath to you which you have made us swear,

18   unless, when we come into the land, you tie this cord of scarlet thread in the window through which you let us down, and gather to yourself into the house your father and your mother and your brothers and all your father's household.

19   "It shall come about that anyone who goes out of the doors of your house into the street, his blood shall be on his own head, and we shall be free; but anyone who is with you in the house, his blood shall be on our head if a hand is laid on him.

20   "But if you tell this business of ours, then we shall be free from the oath which you have made us swear."

21   She said, "According to your words, so be it." So she sent them away, and they departed; and she tied the scarlet cord in the window.

22   They departed and came to the hill country, and remained there for three days until the pursuers returned. Now the pursuers had sought them all along the road, but had not found them.

23   Then the two men returned and came down from the hill country and crossed over and came to Joshua the son of Nun, and they related to him all that had happened to them.

24   They said to Joshua, "Surely the LORD has given all the land into our hands; moreover, all the inhabitants of the land have melted away before us."


### Joshua 6:17-27

17   "The city shall be under the ban, it and all that is in it belongs to the LORD; only Rahab the harlot and all who are with her in the house shall live, because she hid the messengers whom we sent.

18   "But as for you, only keep yourselves from the things under the ban, so that you do not covet them and take some of the things under the ban, and make the camp of Israel accursed and bring trouble on it.

19   "But all the silver and gold and articles of bronze and iron are holy to the LORD; they shall go into the treasury of the LORD."

20   So the people shouted, and priests blew the trumpets; and when the people heard the sound of the trumpet, the people shouted with a great shout and the wall fell down flat, so that the people went up into the city, every man straight ahead, and they took the city.

21   They utterly destroyed everything in the city, both man and woman, young and old, and ox and sheep and donkey, with the edge of the sword.

---

*Notes*

## FYI:

### What's wrong with this picture?

I love Veggie Tales! I have to say this first so you understand I'm commenting here as a fan and not a cranky critic. Even with things we love and trust we need to maintain discernment. If you've seen the Veggie Tales rendition of the fall of Jericho, *Josh and the Big Wall*, you'll know what I mean.

Obviously Veggie Tales gives the text a different spin as they tell their children's versions of classic Bible stories. We know they take liberties in getting the basic story across as they seek to engage kids, but every now and then one of those liberties contradicts the text and when it does, we need to know it and explain it to our kids. We need to help our kids learn to discern truth.

I'm not sure how many times I viewed *Josh and the Big Wall* before it struck me that the inhabitants of Jericho were being entirely misrepresented. While Scripture tells us the people's hearts were melting within them because of fear, the Veggie version portrays pompous French Peas sitting aloft on the wall taunting the marching Israelites because of the strength of their wall. It's funny, but it veers too far.

Does this mean we throw out Veggie Tales? I'm sure not going to, but I always discuss the biblical text when we watch one! Discernment is an everywhere, all-the-time job especially in our culture today.

---

**A BIG PICTURE**
*Guide to the Bible*

## ONE STEP FURTHER:

### Rahab . . .

What else can you learn about Rahab this week? Where will you look? What resources can help you? If you have time, see what you can find. Who is she related to? What do other biblical writers say about her and her faith? Record what you discover in the space below.

22  Joshua said to the two men who had spied out the land, "Go into the harlot's house and bring the woman and all she has out of there, as you have sworn to her."

23  So the young men who were spies went in and brought out Rahab and her father and her mother and her brothers and all she had; they also brought out all her relatives and placed them outside the camp of Israel.

24  They burned the city with fire, and all that was in it. Only the silver and gold, and articles of bronze and iron, they put into the treasury of the house of the LORD.

25  However, Rahab the harlot and her father's household and all she had, Joshua spared; and she has lived in the midst of Israel to this day, for she hid the messengers whom Joshua sent to spy out Jericho.

26  Then Joshua made them take an oath at that time, saying, "Cursed before the LORD is the man who rises up and builds this city Jericho; with the loss of his firstborn he shall lay its foundation, and with the loss of his youngest son he shall set up its gates."

27  So the LORD was with Joshua, and his fame was in all the land.

## DISCUSS with your GROUP or PONDER on your own . . .

Compile a list of everything you learned about Rahab and the people of Jericho.

| Rahab | People of Jericho |
|---|---|
|  |  |

Everyone in Jericho knew that Israel's God was going to win. So what made Rahab different from everyone else?

## ONE STEP FURTHER:

### This may surprise you!

Who was the famous daughter-in-law of Rahab?

What did Rahab do as a result of her faith and how did it affect those around her?

How is your faith affecting others in your circle of influence?

## SETTING the CONTEXT

As mentioned earlier, Judges is a book of tremendous defeat. Throughout its pages, we see cycles of sin, oppression, cries for help, and temporary deliverance. The people of Israel sin. God sends foreign countries to oppress them. Eventually they cry for help and God sends a deliverer-judge to free them from their enemies for a time. When the judge dies, the people start a new cycle. The book shows cycles of sin as well as a linear decline from the beginning to the end.

We see a hint of this at the end of the book of Joshua when we are told, "Israel served the LORD all the days of Joshua and all the days of the elders who survived Joshua, and had known all the deeds of the LORD which He had done for Israel." After Joshua dies, Israel continues to push into the promised land, but they do not completely drive out the inhabitants as God has commanded. And so we are told in Judges 2:19 that with each cycle the people turn back and act more corruptly. The rule of judges comes to an end in the book of 1 Samuel when the people sin even more boldly by asking God, their true King, for a temporal king of flesh and blood to fight their battles. But that, my friend, is a story for another day. Today, we will look at that time of profound decline in the nation of Israel, the time of the judges.

As we work our way through this section, we will look at snippets from the lives of the four men mentioned in Hebrews 11 whose accounts are recorded in Judges: Barak, Gideon, Jephthah, and Samson. We'll save Samuel for next week because he's a hinge character between the judges and the kings.

## OBSERVE the TEXT of SCRIPTURE

We will move through this section chronologically from the Old Testament text which is in a little different order than the one the author of Hebrews has selected.

**READ** Judges 4:1-15. **CIRCLE** every reference to *Barak*, including pronouns, and **UNDERLINE** every reference to *God* and *LORD* watching carefully what He says and does.

### Judges 4:1-15

1    Then the sons of Israel again did evil in the sight of the LORD, after Ehud died.

2    And the LORD sold them into the hand of Jabin king of Canaan, who reigned in Hazor; and the commander of his army was Sisera, who lived in Harosheth-hagoyim.

3    The sons of Israel cried to the LORD; for he had nine hundred iron chariots, and he oppressed the sons of Israel severely for twenty years.

4    Now Deborah, a prophetess, the wife of Lappidoth, was judging Israel at that time.

5    She used to sit under the palm tree of Deborah between Ramah and Bethel in the hill country of Ephraim; and the sons of Israel came up to her for judgment.

6    Now she sent and summoned Barak the son of Abinoam from Kedesh-naphtali, and said to him, "Behold, the LORD, the God of Israel, has commanded, 'Go and march to Mount Tabor, and take with you ten thousand men from the sons of Naphtali and from the sons of Zebulun.

**Notes**

## ONE STEP FURTHER:

### Achan: A Study in Contrasts

If you have time this week, compare and contrast the story of Rahab with the account of Achan. Achan's story is found in Joshua 7. Record your findings below.

As you'll recall from a couple of weeks ago, "Cain killed Abel with the leg of a table." You can add to that the fact that "Achan stole the bacon." I know, I know . . . but you will remember!

7   'I will draw out to you Sisera, the commander of Jabin's army, with his chariots and his many troops to the river Kishon, and I will give him into your hand.' "

8   Then Barak said to her, "If you will go with me, then I will go; but if you will not go with me, I will not go."

9   She said, "I will surely go with you; nevertheless, the honor shall not be yours on the journey that you are about to take, for the LORD will sell Sisera into the hands of a woman." Then Deborah arose and went with Barak to Kedesh.

10  Barak called Zebulun and Naphtali together to Kedesh, and ten thousand men went up with him; Deborah also went up with him.

11  Now Heber the Kenite had separated himself from the Kenites, from the sons of Hobab the father-in-law of Moses, and had pitched his tent as far away as the oak in Zaanannim, which is near Kedesh.

# DIGGING DEEPER
## Pick a Judge

This week, if you have extra time, pick one or two of the judges mentioned in Hebrews 11 and investigate their lives more closely.

What does Judges text tell you about this person? Does it give you background information? Tribe? Upbringing? Family situation? National situation?

What significant events in the life of this judge are recorded? Does this judge have any obvious character flaws? If so, what?

How did this judge begin? How did he live his life? How did he finish?

Once you have studied the texts yourself, you can also consult Bible dictionaries and commentaries to see if they shed any additional light. Record any significant finds below.

What can I learn from this judge to either apply or avoid in my life?

## ONE STEP FURTHER:

**What did he have in mind?**

If you have a little time this week, see if you can find out why the author ordered the judges the way he did.

12  *Then they told Sisera that Barak the son of Abinoam had gone up to Mount Tabor.*

13  *Sisera called together all his chariots, nine hundred iron chariots, and all the people who were with him, from Harosheth-hagoyim to the river Kishon.*

14  *Deborah said to Barak, "Arise! For this is the day in which the LORD has given Sisera into your hands; behold, the LORD has gone out before you." So Barak went down from Mount Tabor with ten thousand men following him.*

15  *The LORD routed Sisera and all his chariots and all his army with the edge of the sword before Barak; and Sisera alighted from his chariot and fled away on foot.*

### DISCUSS with your GROUP or PONDER on your own . . .

What was the situation in Israel during the time of Deborah and Barak?

What extreme advantage did the nations hold over Israel?

Who was Deborah and what did she have to do with Barak?

Look back at every place you marked *God* and *LORD* and recap what role He played in this event from start to finish.

What did God do? What did Barak do? How did Barak act in faith?

## TRUE STORIES:

### Names and Addresses in Judges

| | |
|---|---|
| Barak: | Judges 4–5 |
| Gideon: | Judges 6–8 |
| Jephthah: | Judges 11–12 |
| Samson: | Judges 13–16 |

## FYI:

### Other Mentions

Barak is mentioned in the Bible only in Judges 4-5 and Hebrews 11, Deborah only in the Judges account.

While we're here, consider this: How much does "getting the honor" mean to you? Even when told the honor would go to someone else, Barak still moved forward. What can you apply from this example?

Have you ever become stuck in your walk with God because you hesitated in obedience? What can you learn from Barak about this?

**TRUE STORIES:**

**Deborah and Barak**
This week, get the rest of the story by finishing Judges 4 and reading through the end of Judges 5.

**FYI:**

**How can a commentary help me?**
Commentaries can provide much needed information on the historical background of the biblical text as well as help us enormously in handling the original languages. When faced with a sticky point of interpretation, better commentators will lay out options with the pros and cons for each and then tell you why they support a particular view.

For all the benefit commentaries bring—and there are many—the inherent risk they carry is stunting our own study. Use commentaries wisely *after* you have done your own work, not before!

## GIDEON

### OBSERVE the TEXT of SCRIPTURE

The entire account of Gideon covers Judges 6–8. In Judges 6 God calls a frightened man hiding out in a wine press to deliver an oppressed nation. By Judges 8 we see this man God uses mightily nonetheless finish life poorly. We will pick up in Judges 7 with the story Gideon is most remembered for.

**READ** Judges 7:1-23. **CIRCLE** every reference to *Gideon/Jerubbaal*, including pronouns, and **UNDERLINE** every reference to numbers of people, both for Israel and for her enemies.

*Judges 7:1-23*

1   Then Jerubbaal (that is, Gideon) and all the people who were with him, rose early and camped beside the spring of Harod; and the camp of Midian was on the north side of them by the hill of Moreh in the valley.

2   The LORD said to Gideon, "The people who are with you are too many for Me to give Midian into their hands, for Israel would become boastful, saying, 'My own power has delivered me.'

3   "Now therefore come, proclaim in the hearing of the people, saying, 'Whoever is afraid and trembling, let him return and depart from Mount Gilead.' " So 22,000 people returned, but 10,000 remained.

4   Then the LORD said to Gideon, "The people are still too many; bring them down to the water and I will test them for you there. Therefore it shall be that he of whom I say to you, 'This one shall go with you,' he shall go with you; but everyone of whom I say to you, 'This one shall not go with you,' he shall not go."

5   So he brought the people down to the water. And the LORD said to Gideon, "You shall separate everyone who laps the water with his tongue as a dog laps, as well as everyone who kneels to drink."

*Notes*

6   Now the number of those who lapped, putting their hand to their mouth, was 300 men; but all the rest of the people kneeled to drink water.

7   The LORD said to Gideon, "I will deliver you with the 300 men who lapped and will give the Midianites into your hands; so let all the other people go, each man to his home."

8   So the 300 men took the people's provisions and their trumpets into their hands. And Gideon sent all the other men of Israel, each to his tent, but retained the 300 men; and the camp of Midian was below him in the valley.

9   Now the same night it came about that the LORD said to him, "Arise, go down against the camp, for I have given it into your hands.

10  "But if you are afraid to go down, go with Purah your servant down to the camp,

11  and you will hear what they say; and afterward your hands will be strengthened that you may go down against the camp." So he went with Purah his servant down to the outposts of the army that was in the camp.

12  Now the Midianites and the Amalekites and all the sons of the east were lying in the valley as numerous as locusts; and their camels were without number, as numerous as the sand on the seashore.

13  When Gideon came, behold, a man was relating a dream to his friend. And he said, "Behold, I had a dream; a loaf of barley bread was tumbling into the camp of Midian, and it came to the tent and struck it so that it fell, and turned it upside down so that the tent lay flat."

14  His friend replied, "This is nothing less than the sword of Gideon the son of Joash, a man of Israel; God has given Midian and all the camp into his hand."

15  When Gideon heard the account of the dream and its interpretation, he bowed in worship. He returned to the camp of Israel and said, "Arise, for the LORD has given the camp of Midian into your hands."

16  He divided the 300 men into three companies, and he put trumpets and empty pitchers into the hands of all of them, with torches inside the pitchers.

17  He said to them, "Look at me and do likewise. And behold, when I come to the outskirts of the camp, do as I do.

18  "When I and all who are with me blow the trumpet, then you also blow the trumpets all around the camp and say, 'For the LORD and for Gideon.' "

19  So Gideon and the hundred men who were with him came to the outskirts of the camp at the beginning of the middle watch, when they had just posted the watch; and they blew the trumpets and smashed the pitchers that were in their hands.

20  When the three companies blew the trumpets and broke the pitchers, they held the torches in their left hands and the trumpets in their right hands for blowing, and cried, "A sword for the LORD and for Gideon!"

21  Each stood in his place around the camp; and all the army ran, crying out as they fled.

22  When they blew 300 trumpets, the LORD set the sword of one against another even throughout the whole army; and the army fled as far as Beth-shittah toward Zererah, as far as the edge of Abel-meholah, by Tabbath.

## ONE STEP FURTHER:

**Plot the Slide**

If you have time this week, consider reading the book of Judges and watching the continual downward slide in the behavior of both the people and leaders of Israel. Barak, toward the beginning of this time period, doesn't want to go out unless Deborah goes with him. By the end of Judges, we see tribes of Israel hiring their own priests, priests taking on concubines, and everyone doing what is right in their own eyes.

## TRUE STORIES:

**Gideon**

If you have time this week get the rest of the story about Gideon in Judges 6–8. While you're at it, consider the importance of continuing to walk by faith. God used Gideon to bring about a great deliverance, but he finished life on a sour note. What steps can you take to avoid ending like Gideon?

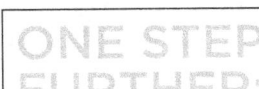

A BIG PICTURE
*Guide to the Bible*

23 *The men of Israel were summoned from Naphtali and Asher and all Manasseh, and they pursued Midian.*

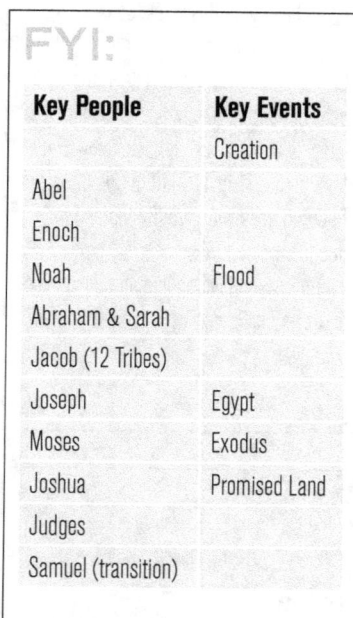

**FYI:**

| Key People | Key Events |
|---|---|
|  | Creation |
| Abel |  |
| Enoch |  |
| Noah | Flood |
| Abraham & Sarah |  |
| Jacob (12 Tribes) |  |
| Joseph | Egypt |
| Moses | Exodus |
| Joshua | Promised Land |
| Judges |  |
| Samuel (transition) |  |

## DISCUSS with your GROUP or PONDER on your own . . .

Why did God tell Gideon he had too many men?

How many men did God whittle it down to? What are we told about the numbers of their opponents?

How did God give Gideon assurance?

What happened when Gideon stepped out in faith with his tiny band of 300 men?

How do you react when you face insurmountable odds? How can this account help you learn to respond in a more God-honoring way?

Spend some time today asking God if there is a specific area in your life where you need to trust Him and move forward by faith in spite of terrible odds.

# DIGGING DEEPER

## Doing a Word Study: Faith, part 3

This week, having taken the time to look at the word *faith* for ourselves, it's now time to see what scholars have to say. Dig into your word study resources such as Strong, Vine, Kittel, Zodhiates, and TWOT. (For information on these resources, see page 111.) Record your findings below.

**ONE STEP FURTHER:**

**The God of Bad Odds**
Just for fun this week, take a little time and record every instance in the Bible that you can recall where God saves or works wonders in the face of overwhelming odds. Then, the next time you are faced with overwhelming odds, remember what you know!!

## JEPHTHAH

### OBSERVE the TEXT of SCRIPTURE

**READ** Judges 11:29-40. **CIRCLE** every reference to *Jephthah*, including pronouns; **UNDERLINE** every reference to *God*; and **BOX** every reference to *Jephthah's daughter*.

*Judges 11:29-40*

29 Now the Spirit of the LORD came upon Jephthah, so that he passed through Gilead and Manasseh; then he passed through Mizpah of Gilead, and from Mizpah of Gilead he went on to the sons of Ammon.

30 Jephthah made a vow to the LORD and said, "If You will indeed give the sons of Ammon into my hand,

31 then it shall be that whatever comes out of the doors of my house to meet me when I return in peace from the sons of Ammon, it shall be the LORD's, and I will offer it up as a burnt offering."

32 So Jephthah crossed over to the sons of Ammon to fight against them; and the LORD gave them into his hand.

33 He struck them with a very great slaughter from Aroer to the entrance of Minnith, twenty cities, and as far as Abel-keramim. So the sons of Ammon were subdued before the sons of Israel.

34 When Jephthah came to his house at Mizpah, behold, his daughter was coming out to meet him with tambourines and with dancing. Now she was his one and only child; besides her he had no son or daughter.

35  When he saw her, he tore his clothes and said, "Alas, my daughter! You have brought me very low, and you are among those who trouble me; for I have given my word to the LORD, and I cannot take it back."

36  So she said to him, "My father, you have given your word to the LORD; do to me as you have said, since the LORD has avenged you of your enemies, the sons of Ammon."

37  She said to her father, "Let this thing be done for me; let me alone two months, that I may go to the mountains and weep because of my virginity, I and my companions."

38  Then he said, "Go." So he sent her away for two months; and she left with her companions, and wept on the mountains because of her virginity.

39  At the end of two months she returned to her father, who did to her according to the vow which he had made; and she had no relations with a man. Thus it became a custom in Israel,

40  that the daughters of Israel went yearly to commemorate the daughter of Jephthah the Gileadite four days in the year.

## ONE STEP FURTHER:

### Problem Promises by Jephthah the Judge

If you're up for a challenge this week, consider the text that says that Jephthah "did to her according to the vow which he had made." This text makes me want to skim over and move on. Is this an instance of human sacrifice in the name of Yahweh in the Old Testament or is it something else? Study the text carefully, check your commentaries, record your findings and give your informed and well-reasoned opinion below.

## DISCUSS with your GROUP or PONDER on your own . . .

What was Jephthah's great victory? What do we learn about the circumstances leading up to it?

What vow did Jephthah make?

What does the text tell us about Jephthah's daughter?

From the entire context, what do you think Jephthah "did" to his daughter and why? List all *your* reasons and then check some commentators to see what they say and why.

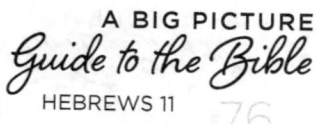

What happened to Jephthah's line after he fulfilled his vow to God? Why?

What can we learn about vows from Jephthah's?

Read the full account of Jephthah in Judges 11–12:7 and list truly commendable acts Jephthah did.

How is your faith standing up against difficult Scriptures? Is God's Word reliable? Explain.

**TRUE STORIES:**

**Jephthah**
This week get the rest of Jephthah's story by reading Judges 11–12.

**ONE STEP FURTHER:**

**So what's a Nazarite?**
Samson is described as a Nazarite from the womb. If you have time, investigate what a "Nazarite" was. Who decided? What were the rules? How did Samson do? Record your discoveries below.

## SAMSON

### SETTING the CONTEXT

One of the more tragic figures in the Bible, Samson is set apart and used by God in spite of himself. He chases foreign women, executes perpetual vengeance on the Philistines he paradoxically loves to hang out with, and behaves egocentrically throughout his life. The most famous story of Samson is his romance with Delilah, the woman who entices him to reveal the secret of his strength. Of course God is the source of his strength, but when Samson tells Delilah of his Nazarite vow and she cuts his hair, his strength leaves him. We pick up Samson's story after this point when the Philistines have captured him in his weakness, put out his eyes, and brought him to a large gathering for their amusement. In the final hours, God strengthens Samson to defeat Israel's enemy.

## OBSERVE the TEXT of SCRIPTURE

**READ** Judges 16:28-31 and **MARK** every reference to *Samson*.

### *Judges 16:28-31*

28  Then Samson called to the LORD and said, "O Lord GOD, please remember me and please strengthen me just this time, O God, that I may at once be avenged of the Philistines for my two eyes."

29  Samson grasped the two middle pillars on which the house rested, and braced himself against them, the one with his right hand and the other with his left.

30  And Samson said, "Let me die with the Philistines!" And he bent with all his might so that the house fell on the lords and all the people who were in it. So the dead whom he killed at his death were more than those whom he killed in his life.

31  Then his brothers and all his father's household came down, took him, brought him up and buried him between Zorah and Eshtaol in the tomb of Manoah his father. Thus he had judged Israel twenty years.

## DISCUSS with your GROUP or PONDER on your own . . .

What did Samson ask God?

How does the story end?

Are you surprised that Samson "makes the cut" for Hebrews 11? Why or why not?

It's very easy to think *our* faith is powerful. Samson is a prime example of God empowering faith within human weakness. *The power is God's, not ours.* Samson was flawed, but God still used him.

While God worked through Samson warts and all, it still makes you wonder what Samson's life could have been had he lived it surrendered to God throughout. If you're alive and reading this, it is not too late to live a life fully surrendered to the God who can work wonders in flawed people!

---

### TRUE STORIES:

**Samson**

Get the rest of Samson's life story by reading Judges 13–16. If you have some extra time, compare Samson's faith with others' listed in Hebrews 11. Record your findings below.

### FYI:

**Listen up!**

A fabulous way to bring God's Word with you throughout the day is to use an audio Bible on your phone. My favorite audio Bible is *The Bible Experience* which is a dramatization of the Scripture from beginning to end. (I listen to this through the Audible app.) Taking the Word in through the ears is a great way to redeem the time. It's also a practical way to help our kids and grandkids learn to dwell in the Word using a familiar delivery method!

What truths can you apply from Samson's life?

## @THE END OF THE DAY . . .

There's nothing like the true accounts of people like Rahab, Barak, Gideon, Jephthah, and Samson to show us God working His purposes through flawed flesh and blood. Although a murderer, Moses still sits on a high mountain, as do Enoch, Abel, Noah, and Abraham. But Rahab? Samson? If God worked through them, He can work through you and me too! Next week, as we transition into the prophets and kings we'll look at one final judge who is a hinge, so to speak, between the judges and kings of Israel. His name? Samuel.

As we close this week, take some time to reflect on what you have studied and ask God to drive specific truths into your heart.

## TAKE ACTION

What specific truth do you need to act on today?

---

THINK ON THIS:

**You Don't Start with the Infield Fly Rule**

Chances are you know what baseball is. Regardless of whether you're a man or a woman, you probably have enough knowledge to explain the very basics of the game to an inquiring child. Now, whether or not you know a little about baseball or a lot about baseball, you'll likely start with things like batters, pitchers, running the bases, balls, strikes, outs, etc. Even if you know what the infield fly rule is [that when a batter hits a pop fly with less than two outs and there is a potential force-out at third or home, the batter is automatically out] the odds you could explain this successfully to a four-year old are minimal—although I must admit I may have done so with my son.

So often we do the equivalent of trying to explain the infield fly rule with people who are new to Bible study. We forget to help them understand the big picture, the balls and strikes and outs, and rather jump into the excruciatingly complex details that can overwhelm beginners.

Is the infield fly rule important? You bet it is, but it will confuse anyone who doesn't know what an out is!

Be encouraged today! Every time you open your Bible and study, you are learning a little bit more and as you walk by the Spirit, your investment will compound over time.

A BIG PICTURE
*Guide to the Bible*

HEBREWS 11

## *Lesson Six*
# The Key to Unlocking the Old Testament

*"Then Ahijah took hold of the new cloak which was on him and tore it into twelve pieces. He said to Jeroboam, 'Take for yourself ten pieces . . .'"*
—1 Kings 11:30-31a

No one understands the Old Testament overnight, but after this lesson you will have enough information to unlock the basic framework. Once you master the basics, you'll have plenty of opportunity to study further, so don't go picking at the details in the sidebars until you have a handle on the big picture. Deal?

And whatever you do, don't be fooled into thinking this is just a dry history lesson! While we are laying the historical grid work (which I must say has all the elements of a major motion picture—sex, money, power) even that is laden with application. So stay in the main text guilt free until you have it down, because once you do you'll have what you need to move forward with clarity.

As you'll recall, we spent our previous lesson looking at Israel after the death of Moses but before the kings. Following Moses' death, Joshua led the people into the promised land. His tenure was marked by extreme success and overwhelming victory. The following years under the judges, however, were a time of defeat and overall corruption that went from bad to worse until the time of Samuel, the last judge, who we will look at today as we make our way into the period of the kings of Israel and Judah.

## FOLLOW UP:

**How are you doing?**
At the end of last week's lesson you identified a truth you needed to act on. How did that go?

## FYI:

| Key People | Key Events |
|---|---|
| | Creation |
| Abel | |
| Enoch | |
| Noah | Flood |
| Abraham & Sarah | |
| Jacob (12 Tribes) | |
| Joseph | Egypt |
| Moses | Exodus |
| Joshua | Promised Land |
| Judges | |
| Samuel (transition) | |
| Saul, David, Solomon | United Kingdom |

## SAMUEL

### OBSERVE the TEXT of SCRIPTURE

Again, the text of Hebrews 11:32 mentions a pair of people in reverse order: David and Samuel. We will follow the Old Testament text chronologically and discuss Samuel first since he was the final judge and was the prophet God called to anoint the first two kings of Israel.

**READ** 1 Samuel 3. **CIRCLE** every reference to *Samuel* and **UNDERLINE** every reference to the *LORD* including pronouns.

### 1 Samuel 3

1    Now the boy Samuel was ministering to the LORD before Eli. And word from the LORD was rare in those days, visions were infrequent.

2    It happened at that time as Eli was lying down in his place (now his eyesight had begun to grow dim and he could not see well),

3    and the lamp of God had not yet gone out, and Samuel was lying down in the temple of the LORD where the ark of God was,

4    that the LORD called Samuel; and he said, "Here I am."

5    Then he ran to Eli and said, "Here I am, for you called me." But he said, "I did not call, lie down again." So he went and lay down.

6    The LORD called yet again, "Samuel!" So Samuel arose and went to Eli and said, "Here I am, for you called me." But he answered, "I did not call, my son, lie down again."

7    Now Samuel did not yet know the LORD, nor had the word of the LORD yet been revealed to him.

8    So the LORD called Samuel again for the third time. And he arose and went to Eli and said, "Here I am, for you called me." Then Eli discerned that the LORD was calling the boy.

9    And Eli said to Samuel, "Go lie down, and it shall be if He calls you, that you shall say, 'Speak, LORD, for Your servant is listening.'" So Samuel went and lay down in his place.

10   Then the LORD came and stood and called as at other times, "Samuel! Samuel!" And Samuel said, "Speak, for Your servant is listening."

11   The LORD said to Samuel, "Behold, I am about to do a thing in Israel at which both ears of everyone who hears it will tingle.

12   "In that day I will carry out against Eli all that I have spoken concerning his house, from beginning to end.

13   "For I have told him that I am about to judge his house forever for the iniquity which he knew, because his sons brought a curse on themselves and he did not rebuke them.

14   "Therefore I have sworn to the house of Eli that the iniquity of Eli's house shall not be atoned for by sacrifice or offering forever."

15   So Samuel lay down until morning. Then he opened the doors of the house of the LORD. But Samuel was afraid to tell the vision to Eli.

16   Then Eli called Samuel and said, "Samuel, my son." And he said, "Here I am."

## ONE STEP FURTHER:

**Mark Eli**

If you have extra time, mark every reference to *Eli* and compile a short list of everything you learn about him.

17  He said, "What is the word that He spoke to you? Please do not hide it from me. May God do so to you, and more also, if you hide anything from me of all the words that He spoke to you."

18  So Samuel told him everything and hid nothing from him. And he said, "It is the LORD; let Him do what seems good to Him."

19  Thus Samuel grew and the LORD was with him and let none of his words fail.

20  All Israel from Dan even to Beersheba knew that Samuel was confirmed as a prophet of the LORD.

21  And the LORD appeared again at Shiloh, because the LORD revealed Himself to Samuel at Shiloh by the word of the LORD.

## DISCUSS with your GROUP or PONDER on your own . . .

What are your initial observations on the text? What questions do you have?

What did you learn about Samuel?

What general age is he?

When did God call Samuel?

How did Samuel respond?

### ONE STEP FURTHER:

**More key words?**

What other words are repeated throughout this passage? If you have some time, identify them and examine their significance. Record your findings below.

How did Eli respond?

How many times did God call before they realized what is going on?

Does the text indicate any reason(s) for this?

If you're aware of Scripture providing additional information, go ahead and cite that here.

When did God finally continue speaking?

Now for the meddling question: How are you at recognizing and hearing the voice of God? How did Samuel's hearing problem differ from Eli's? Do you see any specific application point for your life today? If so, what?

---

### TRUE STORIES:

#### Samuel's Story

Get the rest of the story starting in 1 Samuel 1. Samuel is the last judge of Israel before the people demand a king. His story is found in 1 Samuel. As time allows, do some reading on Samuel and David in 1 and 2 Samuel. Record important information below.

---

The history of faith is one of ups and downs of both heart attitudes and missteps. And while faith is an individual matter, we have also seen the corporate dynamic of people groups exhibiting faith or unbelief. God brings judgment on an unbelieving and sinful world through the flood and spares only righteous Noah and his family. God delivers Israel through a mass exodus from Egypt. Israel's corporate faith in God hits some high points at the exodus and in the early conquests in the promised land, but their faith wanes throughout the days of the judges as the people fail to fully possess the land as God commands.

As we have seen, the people of Israel drift further and further away from God during the period of the judges. Yes, their sin cycles, but each cycle worsens the situation. Eventually, they wear their national heart on their sleeve and ask God to give

them a flesh and blood king. Of course this doesn't take God by surprise. Knowing the demand is coming He warns them beforehand about how kings will treat them. In this next section, we'll take a look at the prediction that the people will ask for a king. We'll watch the people ask and see God's warning before granting their request.

If you are pressed for time, go ahead and proceed to the section entitled **The United Kingdom** (page 89). Background on the kings is important, but the division of the kingdom is what you don't want to miss. I'll summarize the material for you but it will stick much better if you work through it for yourself. In a perfect world, we want it all to stick, right? But according to the last memo I received, we still live in a fallen world. Be encouraged and take one step at a time.

## OBSERVE the TEXT of SCRIPTURE

**READ** Deuteronomy 17:14-20 and **MARK** every reference to *kings* including pronouns. Remember, this was written before Israel took possession of the promised land, before the time of the judges—several hundred years prior to the people asking for a king.

### Deuteronomy 17:14-20

14    "When you enter the land which the LORD your God gives you, and you possess it and live in it, and you say, 'I will set a king over me like all the nations who are around me,'

15    you shall surely set a king over you whom the LORD your God chooses, one from among your countrymen you shall set as king over yourselves; you may not put a foreigner over yourselves who is not your countryman.

16    "Moreover, he shall not multiply horses for himself, nor shall he cause the people to return to Egypt to multiply horses, since the LORD has said to you, 'You shall never again return that way.'

17    "He shall not multiply wives for himself, or else his heart will turn away; nor shall he greatly increase silver and gold for himself.

18    "Now it shall come about when he sits on the throne of his kingdom, he shall write for himself a copy of this law on a scroll in the presence of the Levitical priests.

19    "It shall be with him and he shall read it all the days of his life, that he may learn to fear the LORD his God, by carefully observing all the words of this law and these statutes,

20    that his heart may not be lifted up above his countrymen and that he may not turn aside from the commandment, to the right or the left, so that he and his sons may continue long in his kingdom in the midst of Israel.

## DISCUSS with your GROUP or PONDER on your own . . .

What are your initial observations on the text? What questions do you have?

**FYI:**

| Key People | | Key Events |
|---|---|---|
| | | Creation |
| Abel | | |
| Enoch | | |
| Noah | | Flood |
| Abraham & Sarah | | |
| Jacob (12 Tribes) | | |
| Joseph | | Egypt |
| Moses | | Exodus |
| Joshua | | Promised Land |
| Judges | | |
| Samuel (transition) | | |
| Saul, David, Solomon | | United Kingdom |
| **Judah** | **Israel** | |
| Rehoboam | Jeroboam | |
| Davidic line | Dy*Nasties* | Divided Kingdom |
| Mix of good and bad | All bad | |
| Two Tribes | Ten Tribes | |

A BIG PICTURE
*Guide to the Bible*

When will the people ask for a king?

Why will the people ask for a king? What is the inherent problem in this?

Who may serve as king? What are the requirements?

What is a king NOT supposed to do?

What is a king supposed to do? Why? Who is to be involved?

What does reading the Word daily do? What does this counteract?

As we continue to look at Israel and her kings, it will be very tempting to develop an attitude about what they *didn't* do and what they *should* have done. So let's first consider ourselves in light of these commands. What commands God gave to the kings of Israel are applicable to your life today? (How well do I stay in God's Word? Do I trust power and wealth instead of God? Am I guarding my heart?, etc.) Explain.

QUIZ:

**Write Your Letters**

*(Open book if you need it!)*

Without looking, try writing the first 17 letters of the Greek alphabet with their English equivalents.

1.

2.

3.

4.

5.

6.

7.

8.

9.

10.

11.

12.

13.

14.

15.

16.

17.

# DIGGING DEEPER
## Pulling It All Together

Summarize everything you learned about *faith* from your study so far. What did you learn that you didn't know? What is biblical faith? How does the biblical definition line up with a typical understanding of the word? How would you explain biblical faith to another person? What illustrations would you use to make it clear? Does the visible church today exhibit biblical faith?

## OBSERVE the TEXT of SCRIPTURE

**READ** 1 Samuel 8:7 and 8:10-20. **MARK** every reference to *king* and note what he will do to the people.

### 1 Samuel 8:7

7    The LORD said to Samuel, *"Listen to the voice of the people in regard to all that they say to you, for they have not rejected you, but they have rejected Me from being king over them."*

### 1 Samuel 8:10-20

10    *So Samuel spoke all the words of the LORD to the people who had asked of him a king.*

11    *He said, "This will be the procedure of the king who will reign over you: he will take your sons and place them for himself in his chariots and among his horsemen and they will run before his chariots.*

12    *"He will appoint for himself commanders of thousands and of fifties, and some to do his plowing and to reap his harvest and to make his weapons of war and equipment for his chariots.*

## ONE STEP FURTHER:

**The Complete Greek Alphabet**

| | |
|---|---|
| α | Alpha - "a" |
| β | Beta - "b" |
| γ | Gamma - "g" |
| δ | Delta - "d" |
| ε | Epsilon - short "e" |
| ζ | Zeta - "z" |
| η | Eta - long "a" |
| θ | Theta - "th" |
| ι | Iota - "i" |
| κ | Kappa - "k" |
| λ | Lamda - "l" |
| μ | Mu - "m" |
| ν | Nu - "n" |
| ξ | Xi - "x" |
| o | Omicron - short "o" |
| π | Pi - "p" (pronounced like our letter "p") |
| ρ | Rho - "r" |
| σ | Sigma - "s" |
| τ | Tau - "t" |
| υ | Upsilon - "u" |
| φ | Phi - "ph" (fee) |
| χ | Chi - "x" (xi) |
| ψ | Psi - "ps" (psee) |
| ω | Omega - long "o" |

13   "He will also take your daughters for perfumers and cooks and bakers.

14   "He will take the best of your fields and your vineyards and your olive groves and give them to his servants.

15   "He will take a tenth of your seed and of your vineyards and give to his officers and to his servants.

16   "He will also take your male servants and your female servants and your best young men and your donkeys and use them for his work.

17   "He will take a tenth of your flocks, and you yourselves will become his servants.

18   "Then you will cry out in that day because of your king whom you have chosen for yourselves, but the LORD will not answer you in that day."

19   Nevertheless, the people refused to listen to the voice of Samuel, and they said, "No, but there shall be a king over us,

20   that we also may be like all the nations, that our king may judge us and go out before us and fight our battles."


## DISCUSS with your GROUP or PONDER on your own . . .

What are your initial observations on the text? What questions do you have?

Who were the people *ultimately* rejecting?

What did Samuel warn the people about kings?

How did they respond? Why did they want a king?

Let's be clear here: Who fought Israel's battles to this point? Who brought them out of Egypt? Who delivered them when they cried out? Why were they asking for a king other than the King of kings?

Again, before we criticize too harshly, how often do we opt for what we can see rather than trust our all powerful God who is unseen? What can we learn from their bad example?

## THE UNITED KINGDOM . . . no, not Britain

Samuel anoints one king over Israel who *doesn't* make it into Hebrews 11. His name? Saul. Saul ruled over all 12 tribes of Israel. Although he does relatively well at the outset, he quickly disobeys and God eventually removes him and replaces him with David . . . yes, David of Hebrews 11. Let's look at a couple of David passages before we move to the division of the kingdom. The first you can look up in your own Bible. The second shorter passage, that looks at David's heart, follows on the next page.

## DAVID

## OBSERVE the TEXT of SCRIPTURE

**READ** the account of David's anointing in 1 Samuel 16:1-13 taking note of what God is looking for in the future king.

**READ** Psalm 27:4-8 and **MARK** every reference to the *LORD*.

### Psalm 27:4-8

4    *One thing I have asked from the LORD, that I shall seek: that I may dwell in the house of the LORD all the days of my life, to behold the beauty of the LORD and to meditate in His temple.*

5    *For in the day of trouble He will conceal me in His tabernacle; in the secret place of His tent He will hide me; He will lift me up on a rock.*

6    *And now my head will be lifted up above my enemies around me, and I will offer in His tent sacrifices with shouts of joy; I will sing, yes, I will sing praises to the LORD.*

7    *Hear, O LORD, when I cry with my voice, and be gracious to me and answer me.*

8    *When You said, "Seek My face," my heart said to You, "Your face, O LORD, I shall seek."*

**FYI:**

### Only a Third

It's interesting that Saul, David, and Jeroboam all had the opportunity of enduring kingdoms but only David's lasted. (You can explore the references below this week.) This fact helps us better understand royal succession in both the Northern and Southern Kingdoms.

With Israel still united, Samuel anoints first Saul, then David as king of Israel. After Saul blatantly disobeys clear instruction (1 Samuel 13:13-14) Samuel says to him "the LORD would have established your kingdom over Israel forever. But now your kingdom shall not endure." *Would have established it forever?* That's what the text says.

God replaces King Saul with David whose kingdom does endure (2 Samuel 7:16). With the nation poised to split after the reign of David's son, Solomon, God sends the prophet Ahijah to anoint Jeroboam king of ten tribes. God has already told David his kingdom will endure, so while Jeroboam is given much, God doesn't give it all to him. Because of this promise the Southern Kingdom of Judah has clear succession of kingship within David's bloodlines. Brothers fight for the throne from time to time, but we never see the royal line lost in a coup.

God gives Jeroboam, like Saul and David before him, the opportunity for an enduring house if he obeys (1 Kings 11:38). Jeroboam chooses disobedience and kingship in the North is marked by the instability of ruling houses that cannot endure.

A BIG PICTURE
*Guide to the Bible*
89    HEBREWS 11

## DISCUSS with your GROUP or PONDER on your own . . .

According to 1 Samuel 16, what is God looking for? How does this compare with what man looks at?

---

What happened to David when he was anointed?

---

Turning to Psalm 27, a psalm of David, what did David ask of the Lord? What does this indicate about the condition of his heart?

ONE STEP
FURTHER:

**Promises!**

If you have time, read up on the promises this week!

Saul:          1 Samuel 13:13-14

David:        2 Samuel 7

Jeroboam:  1 Kings 11:28-40

# DIGGING DEEPER
## Who are the rest of the people?

Next week we'll try to identify the remaining unnamed people in Hebrews 11. If you have some time this week, get a jump on this and see what you can find out. Get the general time frame from Hebrews 11. Then see what you can turn up through concordance searches, Bible dictionaries, commentaries, etc. Remember, we never want to be dogmatic where Scripture is not clear, so dig but don't assume God is pipe-lining information just to you. And have fun!

# *Where We Are...*

So let's make sure we have everything straight. **Israel** started off as a **United Kingdom** of 12 tribes descended from **Jacob** (who God renamed Israel). **Joseph** received a double portion so his sons, **Manasseh** and **Ephraim,** basically replace him when the land is handed out, each receiving a full portion along with their uncles (Genesis 48:5, 22). Why don't we see 13 portions of land when we look at maps of ancient Israel? Because the **Levites** did not receive the equivalent of a "state." Instead God scattered them throughout the land in **Levitical cities** and set them apart for His work.

## THE UNITED KINGDOM

God appoints Saul from the tribe of Benjamin to be the first king of Israel. Then he replaces him with David, a man "after [literally 'according to'] His own heart." David was from the tribe of Judah.

David passes the kingdom to his son Solomon, the wisest man at the time (obviously Jesus, the Wisdom of God, supercedes him). Solomon falls into sin and God takes most of the kingdom from his son Rehoboam. Stick with me, we're going to review!! Thereafter, the monarchy becomes a divided kingdom of Israel and Judah. In order to cement this in our minds, we are going to look closely at the life of Solomon and the division of the kingdom. THIS IS WHERE PEOPLE LOSE TRACK OF THE OLD TESTAMENT. So, if you're tired, go get your coffee, take a brisk walk around the block . . . do whatever it takes to focus. This is not difficult, but it takes energy and it's foundational to understanding most of the Old Testament; so lock in with me for the next few pages.

## OBSERVE the TEXT of SCRIPTURE

**READ** 1 Kings 10:23–11:13. If you have colored pencils, **MARK** every reference to *horses* and/or *chariots* in brown. **MARK** every reference to *riches* (*silver, gold,* etc.) in green. **MARK** every reference to *women* (*wives, daughter, princesses,* etc.) in pink. **MARK** every reference to *idols* in black. Or, if you have something against marking, just read the text very carefully keeping these categories in mind.

### *1 Kings 10:23–29*

23  *So King Solomon became greater than all the kings of the earth in riches and in wisdom.*

24  *All the earth was seeking the presence of Solomon, to hear his wisdom which God had put in his heart.*

25  *They brought every man his gift, articles of silver and gold, garments, weapons, spices, horses, and mules, so much year by year.*

26  *Now Solomon gathered chariots and horsemen; and he had 1,400 chariots and 12,000 horsemen, and he stationed them in the chariot cities and with the king in Jerusalem.*

## ONE STEP FURTHER:

**The Davidic Covenant**
If you have some free time this week, look into the Davidic Covenant. What is it and why is it so important?

27  The king made silver as common as stones in Jerusalem, and he made cedars as plentiful as sycamore trees that are in the lowland.

28  Also Solomon's import of horses was from Egypt and Kue, and the king's merchants procured them from Kue for a price.

29  A chariot was imported from Egypt for 600 shekels of silver, and a horse for 150; and by the same means they exported them to all the kings of the Hittites and to the kings of the Arameans.

### 1 Kings 11:1–13

1  Now King Solomon loved many foreign women along with the daughter of Pharaoh: Moabite, Ammonite, Edomite, Sidonian, and Hittite women,

2  from the nations concerning which the LORD had said to the sons of Israel, "You shall not associate with them, nor shall they associate with you, for they will surely turn your heart away after their gods." Solomon held fast to these in love.

3  He had seven hundred wives, princesses, and three hundred concubines, and his wives turned his heart away.

4  For when Solomon was old, his wives turned his heart away after other gods; and his heart was not wholly devoted to the LORD his God, as the heart of David his father had been.

5  For Solomon went after Ashtoreth the goddess of the Sidonians and after Milcom the detestable idol of the Ammonites.

6  Solomon did what was evil in the sight of the LORD, and did not follow the LORD fully, as David his father had done.

7  Then Solomon built a high place for Chemosh the detestable idol of Moab, on the mountain which is east of Jerusalem, and for Molech the detestable idol of the sons of Ammon.

8  Thus also he did for all his foreign wives, who burned incense and sacrificed to their gods.

9  Now the LORD was angry with Solomon because his heart was turned away from the LORD, the God of Israel, who had appeared to him twice,

10  and had commanded him concerning this thing, that he should not go after other gods; but he did not observe what the LORD had commanded.

11  So the LORD said to Solomon, "Because you have done this, and you have not kept My covenant and My statutes, which I have commanded you, I will surely tear the kingdom from you, and will give it to your servant.

12  "Nevertheless I will not do it in your days for the sake of your father David, but I will tear it out of the hand of your son.

13  "However, I will not tear away all the kingdom, but I will give one tribe to your son for the sake of My servant David and for the sake of Jerusalem which I have chosen."

---

*Notes*

---

**FYI:**

**Cheat Sheet**
Here's a quick run down of the events/ time periods and people mentioned so far in Hebrews 11.

**CREATION**
Abel
Enoch
Noah

**FLOOD**
Abraham/Sarah
Isaac
Jacob
Joseph
Moses

**EXODUS**
(Joshua)
Rahab

**JUDGES**
Barak
Gideon
Jephthah
Samson
Samuel (Transition)

**KING**
David

## DISCUSS with your GROUP or PONDER on your own . . .

What are your initial observations on the text? What questions do you have?

Remembering Deuteronomy's commands to kings, what has Solomon violated?

How will God judge Solomon?

What does the Bible tell us about Solomon's wisdom? What can we learn from his life?

What specific lesson can you apply to your life this week from what you learned about Solomon?

## OBSERVE the TEXT of SCRIPTURE

**READ** 1 Kings 11:26-40 three times. The first time through, **MARK** every reference to *Jeroboam*. The second time **MARK** references to *tribes* and anything that represents a tribe (you'll know it when you see it). The third time **MARK** references to *David*.

### *1 Kings 11:26-40*

26    Then Jeroboam the son of Nebat, an Ephraimite of Zeredah, Solomon's servant, whose mother's name was Zeruah, a widow, also rebelled against the king.

27    Now this was the reason why he rebelled against the king: Solomon built the Millo, and closed up the breach of the city of his father David.

*Notes*

28    Now the man Jeroboam was a valiant warrior, and when Solomon saw that the young man was industrious, he appointed him over all the forced labor of the house of Joseph.

29    It came about at that time, when Jeroboam went out of Jerusalem, that the prophet Ahijah the Shilonite found him on the road. Now Ahijah had clothed himself with a new cloak; and both of them were alone in the field.

30    Then Ahijah took hold of the new cloak which was on him and tore it into twelve pieces.

31    He said to Jeroboam, "Take for yourself ten pieces; for thus says the LORD, the God of Israel, 'Behold, I will tear the kingdom out of the hand of Solomon and give you ten tribes

32    (but he will have one tribe, for the sake of My servant David and for the sake of Jerusalem, the city which I have chosen from all the tribes of Israel),

33    because they have forsaken Me, and have worshiped Ashtoreth the goddess of the Sidonians, Chemosh the god of Moab, and Milcom the god of the sons of Ammon; and they have not walked in My ways, doing what is right in My sight and observing My statutes and My ordinances, as his father David did.

34    'Nevertheless I will not take the whole kingdom out of his hand, but I will make him ruler all the days of his life, for the sake of My servant David whom I chose, who observed My commandments and My statutes;

35    but I will take the kingdom from his son's hand and give it to you, even ten tribes.

36    'But to his son I will give one tribe, that My servant David may have a lamp always before Me in Jerusalem, the city where I have chosen for Myself to put My name.

37    'I will take you, and you shall reign over whatever you desire, and you shall be king over Israel.

38    'Then it will be, that if you listen to all that I command you and walk in My ways, and do what is right in My sight by observing My statutes and My commandments, as My servant David did, then I will be with you and build you an enduring house as I built for David, and I will give Israel to you.

39    'Thus I will afflict the descendants of David for this, but not always.' "

40    Solomon sought therefore to put Jeroboam to death; but Jeroboam arose and fled to Egypt to Shishak king of Egypt, and he was in Egypt until the death of Solomon.

## DISCUSS with your GROUP or PONDER on your own . . .

What are your initial observations on the text?

Explain how the kingdom was divided. What visual aid did the prophet use?

What was Jeroboam given? What was he promised?

Why didn't God take it all away from Solomon?

## The Rest of the Story . . .

With **David and Samuel,** the recounting of specific names ends abruptly and we are given instead general terms like **"the prophets"** and **acts of righteousness.** We will look into some of these together and you can investigate the rest in the *Digging Deeper* sections. In the meantime, I want to summarize for you what happens during the time of the unnamed **kings of Israel and Judah.**

In order to make this easy to remember, we're going to fit it with the overall structure of Hebrews 11. At the risk of being repetitive, Israel began as a **United Kingdom.** Her first three kings were **Saul** (of the tribe of Benjamin, who God removed), **David** (of the tribe of Judah), and **Solomon** (David's son).

Because Solomon's heart turned from God, God removed most of the kingdom from the house of David during the time of Solomon's son. He did not take it all away, however, because of His covenant with David. When the author of Hebrews refers to **"David and Samuel and the prophets,"** remember there were other kings in David's line who were men of faith. This line of Davidic kings included both men of faith (Asa, Jehoshaphat, Hezekiah, Josiah) and men of great evil (Manasseh leading the pack).

The **Davidic kings** ruled over Judah, the **Southern Kingdom.** They had levitical priests. Their capital was Jerusalem. They ruled over Judah and Benjamin. Although a stray queen from the north took over for a short time, the land of Judah was ruled by Davidic kings from first to last. Most were men of faith. Perhaps the author of Hebrews has some of these in mind when he refers to David and acts of righteousness. We know some of Judah's kings were men of faith.

The **kings of Israel,** on the other hand, were not. They were not from the line of David and they **ruled over the ten tribes in the north.** They established idol worship and respective priests right from the start. The capital of the north throughout most of its history was **Samaria.** The kings of Israel don't show up in the Hall of Faith, because they were all evil. An exception is Jehu, but for only a short time. The north is marked by coups and a series of evil rulers that knock one another off. I remember this by calling the northern tribes of Israel the land of the **DyNASTIES**—corny perhaps, but memorable.

## @THE END OF THE DAY . . .

As you close out your week of study, spend some time asking God to cement these foundational Old Testament facts into your brain and the truths you have learned from them into your heart. It will help your recall if you explain the basics to a couple of people this week—kids and grandkids are perfect for the job. I've found my kids listen especially well over ice cream.

## TAKE ACTION

Who will you talk to this week about what you've learned?

*Lesson Seven*
# Playing to Win!

> *"Therefore, since we have so great a cloud of witnesses*
> *surrounding us, let us also lay aside every encumbrance and the*
> *sin which so easily entangles us, and let us run with endurance*
> *the race that is set before us . . . "*
> —Hebrews 12:1

Can you believe we've almost finished our course together? For now let's continue running the great course, the race God set before us! In this lesson, we'll consider the "great . . . cloud of witnesses" (Hebrews 12:1) and spend our final moments together studying the "Therefore" of Hebrews 12:1-3. While Hebrews 11 provides a great summary to help us get up to speed on the story of the Bible, it does so much more. The men and women of faith provide us with examples of how to live, how to run, how to follow God fully.

As we near the finish line, we'll also focus on application. What have I learned from the men and women of Hebrews 11? What have I learned about God? How will this impact the choices I make? Based on what I have learned, what encumbrances will I throw off? What sins do I need to ask God to untangle me from?

***What will it take to run with endurance the race that is set before me?***

**FOLLOW UP:**

**How are you doing?**
Did you review the division of the kingdom by telling someone about it? If so, how did it go? If not, there's still time!

## *Where We Are...*

We left off with the division of the kingdom of Israel into the **Northern Kingdom** that retained the name **Israel** and the **Southern Kingdom** known as **Judah**. The north, as you'll remember, had a series of **evil kings** who knocked each other off through coups. If you had enough power and influence in the Northern Kingdom, you could force your way into power. Of course, someone else could throw you out just as easily, but that was life in the north.

The **Southern Kingdom** of Judah, you'll remember, was ruled by **Davidic kings**. The kingship was handed down father to son within bloodlines. This still made for some messes as multiple sons often competed for the throne, but as a whole royal progression was much neater in the south than in the north.

## OBSERVE the TEXT of SCRIPTURE

As we push forward to the end of Hebrews 11 today, you've probably already noticed another shift in the text. The author moves from a focus on specific people to a more general summary of actions and outcomes. Throughout this chapter we have seen a profound emphasis on the "Who," "What," and "When" questions: who accomplished what for the Lord and how? The answer to each is "By faith!" The how emphasis continues in this section, but suddenly the who questions are dropped.

While you could spend time investigating their identities, let's not miss the fact that the author has shifted. Let's not pick too closely for details when he is turning our heads another direction. He is going in for a close that will cause us again to remember that the emphasis of the chapter is faith. His purpose is not to deify examples but to use them to spur readers on to similar lives of faith!

**READ** Hebrews 11:32-40. Although we've already looked at verse 32, it is included here to pick up the full sentence and make sure you understand the context and continuity of thought. As you read, **UNDERLINE** "good" outcomes and **CIRCLE** "bad" ones.

### *Hebrews 11:32-40*

32   *And what more shall I say? For time will fail me if I tell of Gideon, Barak, Samson, Jephthah, of David and Samuel and the prophets,*

33   *who by faith conquered kingdoms, performed acts of righteousness, obtained promises, shut the mouths of lions,*

34   *quenched the power of fire, escaped the edge of the sword, from weakness were made strong, became mighty in war, put foreign armies to flight.*

35   *Women received back their dead by resurrection; and others were tortured, not accepting their release, so that they might obtain a better resurrection;*

---

## FYI:

**The DyNASTIES of Israel**

The kings of Israel didn't make the cut for the faith chapter because they were not men of faith. Still, we can learn much from them about what NOT to do!

Here's a way to remember the big picture of the DyNASTIES of Israel. We'll use the name of the father of each DyNASTY to help us recall the whole group. These obviously are not last names, just mnemonic tools.

**The JEROBOAMs . . .**

      Jeroboam (tribe of Ephraim)
      Nadab
COUP —  Baasha (tribe of Issachar) takes over Elah
COUP —  Zimri takes over but is almost immediately taken down by the people who raise up Omri.

**The OMRIs . . .**

      Omri
      Ahab
      Ahaziah
      Jehoram (another son of Ahab as Ahaziah had no son)

**The JEHUs . . .**

      Jehu takes over by conspiracy, but God anoints him king
      Jehoahaz
      Joash
      Jeroboam 2
      Zechariah
COUP —  Shallum
COUP —  Menahem
      Pekahiah
COUP —  Pekah
COUP —  Hoshea

**THE NORTHERN KINGDOM FALLS TO ASSYRIA IN 722 BC**

A BIG PICTURE
*Guide to the Bible*

36 and others experienced mockings and scourgings, yes, also chains and imprisonment.

37 They were stoned, they were sawn in two, they were tempted, they were put to death with the sword; they went about in sheepskins, in goatskins, being destitute, afflicted, ill-treated

38 (men of whom the world was not worthy), wandering in deserts and mountains and caves and holes in the ground.

39 And all these, having gained approval through their faith, did not receive what was promised,

40 because God had provided something better for us, so that apart from us they would not be made perfect.

## DISCUSS with your GROUP or PONDER on your own . . .

What are your initial observations on the text?

What questions do you have?

At what point does the text take a dramatic turn? What does it turn to?

Look back at your markings and compile a simple list of the "good" and "bad" outcomes. Don't forget to record the verses.

| GOOD | BAD |
|------|-----|
|      |     |
|      |     |
|      |     |
|      |     |

### ONE STEP FURTHER:

**Jeroboam—The Progression of Unbelief**

If you have some extra time this week, consider the accounts of Jeroboam from 1 Kings 11:34-39 and 12:25-33. As you read, note God's promise to Jeroboam and the subsequent downward progression of his thought processes as unbelief rules in his heart and mind. Thoughts to consider while you read:

– What did God promise to Jeroboam?

– What did Jeroboam fear?

– How did Jeroboam's fear snowball?

– How can we guard against "pulling a Jeroboam"?

### ONE STEP FURTHER:

**Them and Us**

"Apart from us they would not be made perfect" (Hebrews 11:40). What does this mean and why does it matter? What is the "something better" God provided for us? If you have some extra time this week, explore these questions and record your findings below.

## FYI:

### Naming Some of the Unnamed

While we don't know who the author of Hebrews had in mind when he lists only actions, here are a few whose lives fit some of the descriptions.

**33**

shut the mouths of lions - *Daniel*

**34**

quenched the power of fire - *Shadrach, Meshach, Abednego*

escaped the edge of the sword - *Elijah, Elisha, Jeremiah*

from weakness were made strong - *David, Samson, Gideon*

**35**

women received back their dead by resurrection - *probably a reference to the resurrections through Elijah and Elisha*

others were tortured, not accepting their release - *may be a reference to persecutions during the Maccabean period*

**37-38**

stoned - *tradition points to Jeremiah*

sawn in two - *traditionally this is associated with Isaiah*

went about in sheepskins, in goatskins, being destitute, afflicted, ill-treated, wandering in deserts and mountains and caves and holes in the ground - *could include Elijah, Elisha, Ezekiel, and John the Baptist*

## TRUE STORIES:

### Elijah and Elisha

God used both of these prophets to bring people back from the dead. You can read about Elijah and Elisha in 1 and 2 Kings.

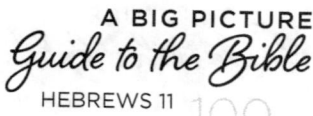
---

Lesson Seven: **Playing to Win!**

Do the final verses of Hebrews 11 evoke a different response in you than the earlier part of the chapter? Why or why not?

How are the outcomes at the end of the chapter different from the earlier ones?

In what ways are all the outcomes similar?

Is living by faith different when life is difficult? Support your answer with specific examples from your life.

What have you learned by walking with men and women of faith?

Has your faith influenced others? Explain.

The men and women of faith who died before the cross looked forward to the promise of a Messiah-Savior. Some saw lesser promises and miracles fulfilled, but they all "gained approval" through their faith, though they died (with the exception of Enoch!) without receiving the promises during their mortal lifetimes.

## OBSERVE the TEXT of SCRIPTURE

**READ** Hebrews 12:1-3 and **MARK** every reference to *endurance*.

*Hebrews 12:1-3*

1   *Therefore, since we have so great a cloud of witnesses surrounding us, let us also lay aside every encumbrance and the sin which so easily entangles us, and let us run with endurance the race that is set before us,*

2   *fixing our eyes on Jesus, the author and perfecter of faith, who for the joy set before Him endured the cross, despising the shame, and has sat down at the right hand of the throne of God.*

3   *For consider Him who has endured such hostility by sinners against Himself, so that you will not grow weary and lose heart.*

## DISCUSS with your GROUP or PONDER on your own . . .

What are your initial observations on the text?

What questions do you have?

What words and phrases can you focus on for further study?

What words tie these verses to the overall theme of Hebrews 11 and how do they function?

What specific actions is the author of Hebrews calling us to?

---

FYI:

**How the Prophets Fit with the Redemption Story**

One of the reasons the Bible can seem so unwieldy stems from the different genres of literature it contains. Because the Scriptures mix historical narrative, poetry, wisdom literature, and prophecies we modern readers often don't know which way is up. Poetry and wisdom literature can come across like stand-alone sidebars while prophetic books stir history and mystery together that can quickly create confusion. So how do we solve the problem?

Stick with the main story as you start. When we understand the Bible's basic theme weaved through the historical narrative sections, we can see where the poetry, wisdom literature, and prophecy fit along the way.

In the end, everything points to God's saving work in Jesus. Get "the" story first and you'll more easily understand the prophets. Easy, of course is a relative term, but hey, a little challenge is a good thing!!

---

**A BIG PICTURE**
*Guide to the Bible*

How can we accomplish them?

QUIZ:

**Write Your Letters**

*(Open book if you need it!)*

Recite your Greek alphabet on paper!

1.
2.
3.
4.
5.
6.
7.
8.
9.
10.
11.
12.
13.
14.
15.
16.
17.
18.
19.
20.
21.
22.
23.
24.

Now for the hard stuff. Be quiet before God and ask Him to reveal to you any sins or encumbrances in your life. You may want to go for a walk, just get alone and listen. Chances are you have an idea about some of these, but others are sitting in blind spots.

Is a habitual sin preventing you from running the race before you? If there is, talk to God about it and ask Him to give you wisdom and power to overcome it. Depending on your struggle, you may benefit by sharing your journey with another person.

Write down whatever you need to remember. What encumbrances are you lugging around? Remember, an encumbrance is not necessarily bad in itself; it is just something that weighs you down. It may be something out of balance. It may be a responsibility you take on that belongs to someone else. Focusing on a goal almost always goes hand in hand with running lighter. Running lighter has everything to do with identifying and throwing off encumbrances. So while you may not have felt comfortable writing down specific areas of sin above, I strongly encourage you to record the encumbrances that keep you from running your best race as a first step toward running lighter.

Before you move on, ask yourself these questions to see if you can identify other encumbrances:

- *What do I spend time on that someone else could do at 80% of my efficiency?*
- *What am I watching on TV? How much time do I spend per week?*
- *What am I reading? How much time do I spend per week?*
- *How much time do I spend on the Internet or with e-mail per week?*
- *How much time do I spend on activities and tasks that are not my direct responsibility?*
- *How often do I say "Yes" to requests I am not gifted for when I should say "No"?*
- *Are there simple decisions I can make that will save me time? (For example: buying more wrinkle-free clothes, etc.; deciding not to feel guilty if I make a cake out of a box; having someone else change the oil.)*
- *What avoidable situations in life cost me in mental energy and stress?*

Sorry for meddling. Record any additional thoughts below.

What does the author of Hebrews exhort us to do with our eyes in Hebrews 12? How does this vision compare with the vision of the men and women of faith in Hebrews 11?

What steps will you take this week to throw off encumbrances and sin in your life? (The more specific you can be the better.)

Remember, my friend, as we seek to throw off encumbrances and sin and to run the race set before us, we do it by faith! It is not something we muster up on our own, we are empowered by the One who set us free from the power of death! As we bring our study to a close, we are going to dip back into Hebrews 2 for a reminder of why we can walk in faith and whose aid we can count on when times are dark and temptations abound.

## OBSERVE the TEXT of SCRIPTURE

READ Hebrews 2:9-18 and MARK every reference to *Jesus*.

### Hebrews 2:9-18

9  *But we do see Him who was made for a little while lower than the angels, namely, Jesus, because of the suffering of death crowned with glory and honor, so that by the grace of God He might taste death for everyone.*

10  *For it was fitting for Him, for whom are all things, and through whom are all things, in bringing many sons to glory, to perfect the author of their salvation through sufferings.*

11  *For both He who sanctifies and those who are sanctified are all from one Father; for which reason He is not ashamed to call them brethren,*

12  *saying, "I WILL PROCLAIM YOUR NAME TO MY BRETHREN, IN THE MIDST OF THE CONGREGATION I WILL SING YOUR PRAISE."*

13  *And again, "I WILL PUT MY TRUST IN HIM." And again, "BEHOLD, I AND THE CHILDREN WHOM GOD HAS GIVEN ME."*

14  *Therefore, since the children share in flesh and blood, He Himself likewise also partook of the same, that through death He might render powerless him who had the power of death, that is, the devil,*

15  *and might free those who through fear of death were subject to slavery all their lives.*

16  *For assuredly He does not give help to angels, but He gives help to the descendant of Abraham.*

### ONE STEP FURTHER:

**Consider . . .**

If you have time this week, consider everything that the people of Hebrews 11 considered. As you do so, consider the different Greek words behind the English word *consider*. Record your findings below.

### ONE STEP FURTHER:

**The Power of Death**

What power over death did the devil hold and why? Take some time this week to explore this question on your own before consulting secondary sources.

17  *Therefore, He had to be made like His brethren in all things, so that He might become a merciful and faithful high priest in things pertaining to God, to make propitiation for the sins of the people.*

18  *For since He Himself was tempted in that which He has suffered, He is able to come to the aid of those who are tempted.*

## DISCUSS with your GROUP or PONDER on your own . . .

What are your initial observations on the text?

Based on your markings, compile a list of everything you learned about Jesus from this passage.

What does the text tell us about man's condition? How did Jesus change this?

What benefits do we have that those who lived in faith before the cross could only look forward to and welcome from a distance?

How does this passage address the solution to our sin problem?

Does this passage address our encumbrance problem as well? Explain.

There's another frequent word in this passage we can't overlook. It is *death*. How does Jesus' death free us from the fear of death? What impact does freedom from the fear of death have on walking the life of faith?

# DIGGING DEEPER
## Why is there so much talk about death in a chapter on faith?

Faith absolutely dominates Hebrews 11, but there is also an awful lot of talk about death. If you have a chance this week, spend some time digging to find out why so much death talk would show up in a chapter on faith.

What are your initial observations on the usage of *death* in Hebrews 11?

Where are *death* words (*death, died, dying,* etc.) used in this passage? Who are they referring to?

How does the human condition of mortality play into this chapter? Did the people get what they were looking for during this lifetime? If not, what does that suggest about the true duration of life?

How can people's views of death impact their walks of faith and how they do life?

What else have you learned from your study?

How will you apply what you've learned?

ONE STEP FURTHER:

**"A Better Resurrection"?**
Wait a minute, what's this all about? Think this through carefully based on the full context of Scripture. Then check commentaries and record your findings below. (Hint: think about the kinds of resurrections talked about in the immediate context!)

# DIGGING DEEPER
## How do I endure?

What does *endurance* mean and, more importantly, how can I *endure* in the midst of life's trials and circumstances? Use your concordance to locate other occurrences of *endure*, *endurance*, and synonyms. Record what you learn from your observations and then compare your findings with those of commentators as you draw your conclusions.

How are these words used in the book of Hebrews?

Where else do we see these words used in the New Testament?

Is this idea throughout the Bible or is it just a favorite of the author of Hebrews? Explain

What have you learned by looking at the usage of these words?

What do your resources tell you about how these words were used in the LXX (See FYI box) and the Greek world?

What other items of interest did you find?

How does the writer of Hebrews picture endurance?

## ONE STEP FURTHER:

### Word Study: *Witness*

Examine the word for *witness* in Hebrews 12:1. What is the Greek word and where else have we seen it in this study? Record your findings below.

## ONE STEP FURTHER:

### Sins and Encumbrances

Spend some time studying and considering the similarities and differences between sins and encumbrances. Record your findings below.

Would those who know you best say your life is characterized by faith or fear? Explain.

Spend some time today with God and ask Him to reveal any fears you're harboring in your life and to replace them with faith. Record any pertinent thoughts.

## @THE END OF THE DAY . . .

So where do you fit in? Where do I fit in? Hebrews 11 presents us with an excellent summary of the biblical story of redemption but it also leaves us with a profound challenge. Will you, will I, pick up the baton and run the race as those who have gone before, not in our own power but in His by faith? Generations have known about Abel, Noah, Abraham, Sarah, Isaac, Jacob, Joseph, Moses, Rahab, and the rest. But the story doesn't end with them! God's story continues in you and in me. No, our faith will never be recorded in holy writ, but our lives are a part of the continuum of faith; we are among those apart from whom the Old Testament faithful will not be made perfect.

My friend, we run with the advantage of a clear goal. We are called to fix our eyes on Jesus. We run having examples of faith who now surround us as "so great a cloud of witnesses."

What is the next step of faith that God is calling you to today? Don't worry about a mile down the path. Right now, record what you think is the next single step He is calling you to.

Are sins hampering your obedience and your ability to hear His voice? If so, what steps will you take to align yourself with God's revealed truth?

What encumbrances are weighing you down and holding you back from running your best race? How will you run lighter?

### FYI:

**Are you being perfected by the flesh?**

"You foolish Galatians, who has bewitched you, before whose eyes Jesus Christ was publicly portrayed *as* crucified? This is the only thing I want to find out from you: did you receive the Spirit by the works of the Law, or by hearing with faith? Are you so foolish? Having begun by the Spirit, are you now being perfected by the flesh?"

—Galatians 3:1-3

### ONE STEP FURTHER:

**John 15**

Spend some time this week soaking in John 15 and considering how a tree bears fruit and how this applies to our lives as believers in Christ and to our walk of faith. Record your findings below.

## How will your faith be recorded?

By faith Abel offered a better sacrifice.

By faith Enoch was pleasing to God.

By faith Noah prepared an ark.

By faith Abraham when he was called, obeyed.

By faith Sarah received ability to conceive.

By faith Abraham offered up Isaac.

By faith Isaac blessed Jacob and Esau.

By faith Jacob blessed each of the sons of Joseph.

By faith Joseph made mention of the exodus.

By faith Moses considered the reproach of Christ greater riches than the treasures of Egypt.

By faith Rahab welcomed the spies in peace.


By faith _____ , (your name here)
not being weighed down by encumbrances or entangled by sin,

_____

_____

_____

_____ .


*"Now to Him who is able to keep you from stumbling, and to make you stand in the presence of His glory blameless with great joy, to the only God our Savior, through Jesus Christ our Lord, be glory, majesty, dominion and authority, before all time and now and forever. Amen."*
—Jude 24-25

**ONE STEP FURTHER:**

**Here's the Post-Test!**
Take a few minutes and list to the best of your ability the major characters you've learned about while studying Hebrews 11.

# RESOURCES

## Helpful Study Tools

*The New How to Study Your Bible*
Eugene, Oregon: Harvest House
Publishers

*The New Inductive Study Bible*
Eugene, Oregon: Harvest House
Publishers

*Logos Bible Software*
Available at www.logos.com.

## Greek Word Study Tools

Kittel, G., Friedrich, G.,
& Bromiley, G.W.
*Theological Dictionary of the New
Testament, Abridged* (also known as
Little Kittel)
Grand Rapids, Michigan: W.B.
Eerdmans Publishing Company

Zodhiates, Spiros
*The Complete Word Study Dictionary:
New Testament*
Chattanooga, Tennessee: AMG
Publishers

## Hebrew Word Study Tools

Harris, R.L., Archer, G.L.,
& Walker, B.K.
*Theological Wordbook of the Old
Testament* (also known as TWOT)
Chicago, Illinois: Moody Press

Zodhiates, Spiros
*The Complete Word Study Dictionary:
Old Testament*
Chattanooga, Tennessee: AMG
Publishers

## General Word Study Tools

Strong, James
*The New Strong's Exhaustive
Concordance of the Bible*
Nashville, Tennessee: Thomas Nelson

## Recommended Commentary Sets

*Expositor's Bible Commentary*
Grand Rapids, Michigan: Zondervan

*NIV Application Commentary*
Grand Rapids, Michigan: Zondervan

*The New American Commentary*
Nashville, Tennessee: Broadman and
Holman Publishers

## Advanced Commentary on Hebrews

Ellingworth, Paul
*The Epistle to the Hebrews: A
Commentary on the Greek Text*
Grand Rapids, MI: W.B. Eerdmans
Publishing Company

# We'd Love to Hear From You!

If you found this study helpful please take

a moment to share your thoughts.

## Leave a Review

https://www.pamgillaspieshop.com/products/hebrews-11-big-picture-guide-to-the-bible

OR

## Take a Short Survey

https://bit.ly/Hebrews11BookSurvey

www.ingramcontent.com/pod-product-compliance
Lightning Source LLC
Chambersburg PA
CBHW081337120626
46546CB00011B/3381